SUCCESSFUL EARLY YEARS OFSTED INSPECTIONS

SAGE was founded in 1965 by Sara Miller McCune to support the dissemination of usable knowledge by publishing innovative and high-quality research and teaching content. Today, we publish over 900 journals, including those of more than 400 learned societies, more than 800 new books per year, and a growing range of library products including archives, data, case studies, reports, and video. SAGE remains majority-owned by our founder, and after Sara's lifetime will become owned by a charitable trust that secures our continued independence.

Los Angeles | London | New Delhi | Singapore | Washington DC | Melbourne

JULIAN GRENIER

SUCCESSFUL EARLY YEARS OFSTED INSPECTIONS

THRIVING CHILDREN, CONFIDENT STAFF

Los Angeles | London | New Delhi
Singapore | Washington DC | Melbourne

Los Angeles | London | New Delhi
Singapore | Washington DC | Melbourne

SAGE Publications Ltd
1 Oliver's Yard
55 City Road
London EC1Y 1SP

SAGE Publications Inc.
2455 Teller Road
Thousand Oaks, California 91320

SAGE Publications India Pvt Ltd
B 1/I 1 Mohan Cooperative Industrial Area
Mathura Road
New Delhi 110 044

SAGE Publications Asia-Pacific Pte Ltd
3 Church Street
#10-04 Samsung Hub
Singapore 049483

Editor: Jude Bowen
Assistant editor: George Knowles
Production editor: Tom Bedford
Copyeditor: Andy Baxter
Indexer: Cathy Heath
Marketing manager: Dilhara Attygalle
Cover design: Wendy Scott
Typeset by: C&M Digitals (P) Ltd, Chennai, India
Printed and bound by CPI Group (UK) Ltd,
Croydon, CR0 4YY

© Julian Grenier 2017

First published 2017

Library of Congress Control Number: 2016939627

British Library Cataloguing in Publication data

A catalogue record for this book is available from
the British Library

ISBN 978-1-4739-3840-3
ISBN 978-1-4739-3841-0 (pbk)

CONTENTS

About the Author

© Maisie Vollans

Julian Grenier is the Headteacher of Sheringham Nursery School and Children's Centre in Newham, East London, rated 'Outstanding' twice by Ofsted in 2014 and a National Teaching School.

Julian has worked in the early years for the last two decades as teacher, Special Educational Needs Co-ordinator, headteacher and as Senior Early Years Adviser to the London Borough of Tower Hamlets. He has been the National Chair of Early Education, and was a member of the advisory groups for the Nutbrown Review of Early Education and Childcare Qualifications and the Rose Review of the Primary Curriculum.

Julian has a Doctorate in Education from the UCL Institute of Education, London, gained for his research into the work, views and theories of early years practitioners working with two-year-olds. He is a National Leader of Education and a trustee of the East London Partnership, which brings together schools, early years settings and childminders to work collaboratively, improve quality and enhance the life chances of young children in East London.

Julian is the co-author of the best-selling *Child Care and Education* (5th edition) with Tina Bruce and Carolyn Meggitt.

@juliangrenier

www.juliangrenier.blogspot.com

PREFACE

This book provides navigational tools which help leaders and managers of early childhood practice, working in a range of settings, to find their way through the complexities of the work they do, and to deepen their sense of fulfilment in working with the children, families and staff as well as the challenges they deal with daily.

The information presented has great clarity and is very accessible to read. There is enjoyable provocation towards thought and reflection, with practical guidance to help leaders and managers into 'discussion, debate and professional dialogue' with staff and families.

Whilst acknowledging Ofsted's importance, the book sets the inspectorate in a contextualised framework such that 'the tail does not wag the dog', and it shows the pitfalls of responding to 'every fashion, whim or headline'. The case studies provide invaluable help in developing and sustaining quality of practice, so that children are given of the best in this short but important phase of their lives. This book will guide, support and help the reader to be strong through their journey.

Tina Bruce, CBE

ACKNOWLEDGEMENTS

I would like to thank the following for their help and support throughout the writing of this book.

Everyone on the team at Sheringham Nursery School and Children's Centre, with particular thanks to Lesley Webb and Rehema Essop. Thanks also to Rebekah Iiyambo. I am very grateful to Sue for her insightful and helpful notes during the writing process.

However, the book expresses my own views and opinions and I am responsible for any errors.

Thanks to Tina Bruce, who first inspired me to think about early childhood, play and learning many years ago as a young deputy headteacher, and to Liz Brooker at the Institute of Education for seven years of supervision and support.

I am indebted to Professor Simon Holmes and the Maxillofacial Surgery Team at Barts Health.

It has been a pleasure to work with Jude Bowen, George Knowles and Amy Jarrold at SAGE to develop the book.

Finally, special thanks to Caroline for putting up with it, and me.

COMPANION WEBSITE

This book is accompanied by free downloadable material. Each time you see the following icon ➤, head over to https://study.sagepub.com/grenier to download an editable version of the document.

☆

PART 1

DEVELOPING THE PROFESSIONALISM, SKILLS AND CONFIDENCE OF YOUR STAFF TEAM

☆

1

Introduction

It has never been more important to have a successful Ofsted. If you are an early years setting, you may lose local authority funding for some of your places unless you are judged to be 'Good' or 'Outstanding'. Many parents who pay for childcare will look around first using the Ofsted website, and may rule out anywhere that does not have a positive report. It will also be much harder to recruit good staff if you have been judged as a setting which 'Requires Improvement' or is 'Inadequate'.

If you are in a maintained school, there are equal, if different, pressures. The specific early years judgement in the new school inspection framework means that a poor outcome for children in the Early Years Foundation Stage (EYFS) could bring down the school's overall grade. Ofsted have focussed strongly in recent years on transition in the early years, progress and specifically the outcomes of children eligible for free school meals: shortcomings in any of these areas could have a very adverse effect on Ofsted's overall judgement of the school.

For both schools and settings, the judgement that you Require Improvement will lead to more regular monitoring and inspection. Being found Inadequate will lead to intense pressure: schools may be forced into academies or federations, and settings may lose their registration, if they do not manage to improve rapidly. Complaints or concerns that you are failing to meet the Statutory Framework for the EYFS can also trigger no-notice inspections and lead to a poor grade, even for a school or setting which has previously been successful.

So, it may come as a surprise that, although this book is about achieving success in your Ofsted inspection, it does not take Ofsted, or its current inspection frameworks, as the final word in best practice. For a start, those frameworks, reports and public announcements change significantly from one year to the next, depending on a whole range of other priorities, including the personal views of the Chief Inspector of Schools. In this book, I am arguing that whilst Ofsted is important, we must not allow the tail to wag the dog. What really matters is that we find ways to develop safe, effective and sustainable early years practice which meets the needs of the children and families we work with.

We need to grow staff teams so that individuals work well together and develop their professionalism. And we need a range of techniques to collect information about how effective our practice is, so that we are constantly monitoring the quality of the provision and the children's progress and wellbeing, and making adjustments where necessary. These cycles of development should be robust and accurate, and we should be open with staff and with parents about how well we are doing and what we need to do to get better. Most importantly, we need to work together, as professionals, to develop the values and principles which will guide our work. No-one ever journeyed far by changing course every few moments, and no-one can offer children a high-quality experience of early education by making changes according to every fashion, whim or headline.

That said, Ofsted itself has consistently argued for some important principles: that children in disadvantaged circumstances should have the care and teaching they need, so that they have as good a chance to do well in their education as their more advantaged peers; that children should be kept safe and healthy; and that staff should be professionally led and managed so that they can develop their skills and professionalism. Until a few decades ago, the regulation of early years settings was locally determined and inconsistent. Ofsted took over in 2000, and Peter Elfer has argued that there is evidence to suggest that there has been:

> a significant improvement in the safety of nurseries compared to before 2000, when inspection and enforcement were much weaker. Alongside improvements in safety, regulation has also ensured that awareness of the importance of emotional well-being and the provision of a broad range of opportunities for play and learning is commonplace. (Elfer, 2014: 288)

On the other hand, the pressure which is created by Ofsted's no-notice and short-notice inspection regimes can lead to a defensive culture. Managers and staff set about trying to please Ofsted: decisions are taken on the basis of second-guessing what an Ofsted inspector may wish to see. In my role as a senior early years adviser, I would often ask staff why they used a particular format for their planning, or timetabled the day in a certain way, and would get a two-word answer: 'For Ofsted.' However, in this book, Ofsted's framework and inspection system is not seen as a guide to best practice, but rather as a way for you and your setting to validate your practice, and to be accountable for the public money which you receive. Successive governments have invested many billions of pounds in early years provision: just think about all the Children's Centres which have been built, the expansion of free places for two-, three- and four-year-olds, and funding for staff training and development over the years. The public is entitled to know whether these are wise investments, and Ofsted is the main source the public rely on for this information.

It is also important not to see Ofsted as the only indicator of quality. Academics like Professors Iram Siraj, Kathy Sylva and Ted Melhuish, who spend their working lives researching the quality of early years provision and looking at what promotes the best outcomes for children, have consistently argued that it is important to have a range of tools to assess quality. It is also important to have well-trained, confident and skilful professionals who can make judgements which are specific to their school, setting or community. There is no 'manual' that can teach any of us how to be the perfect carer or teacher: but high-quality training, reflection on our work and experiences, and working in supportive teams can help us to get better throughout our careers.

It is difficult to make decisions about measuring outcomes and measuring quality: difficult, but essential if we are to make a difference. We need to make those decisions as well as we can, using the best available information, and as openly as possible by engaging and involving staff, parents and other stakeholders.

Having a range of perspectives on quality cannot just mean considering a lot of different opinions: instead, we need tools and approaches that can provide us with useful information or 'data' about how well we are achieving the aims which we have set out. The choice of tools to use will depend on how well developed your provision is. Later in this book, assessing your setting's level of development and the tools you might use to help you in self-evaluation are discussed in more detail. Drawing on an approach which was first developed by Pauline Hoare, Early Years Lead Officer in the London Borough of Tower Hamlets, I am proposing that there are three broad phases of development in the journey towards the most effective and appropriate practice.

Phase one: Practice which works for you

If you are leading a new team, or you are struggling to achieve a satisfactory level of quality and consistency, then you will need to focus on meeting the requirements of the Statutory Framework for the EYFS. You may need to insist on a high level of documentation: you will need to see plans for adult-guided learning and for child-initiated play opportunities that detail resourcing, strategies for adults to follow, and learning outcomes for the children to check that they are at least adequate. You may need to lay down a requirement for the number of observations and assessments to be completed per week, and to see how these assessments inform the weekly planning. By linking these with your monitoring observations and monitoring of the outcomes for children, you will be able to begin to establish what works for you. This includes having evidence to show it works: evidence that this approach is supporting a good quality of adult care and interaction, and that it is effective in supporting the development and wellbeing of the children on roll so that each child makes good progress in their learning.

Phase two: Practice which works for you, and is consistent with the research and evidence base

Once you are confident that you have achieved a level of consistency in the team's practice, and that this is effective for the children on roll, you will need to develop further by looking beyond your individual setting. On our own, we can only achieve a certain amount: we need to learn from the practice and insights of others, rather than trying to create everything from scratch.

For example, you may be able to show that staff are interacting positively with children and focussing on listening to them and holding conversations. To develop your practice further, you could then adopt an evidence-based programme like the Early Talk 0–5 years programme from I CAN, the National Communication Charity (www.ican.org.uk/ICAN-Training/Early/Early%20 Talk%200-5.aspx). There is a good evidence base to suggest that this programme can enhance the learning environment for all children and can have a long-term and positive impact on staff and practice.

When your staff team is more highly trained and skilled in their practice, and you can show that outcomes for children are good, then you will not need so much written or documented evidence. An inexperienced or little-trained member of staff may need a plan before an activity, detailing what she or he will say to the children and how conversation will be encouraged. You may need to check this plan to ensure that an appropriate experience will be offered. But, in the case of a more highly trained member of staff, whose practice you have observed to be effective, you will not need to see this level of detail because you can rely on her or his professional judgement and skill.

Phase three: Developing leading-edge practice

A well-trained and highly professional staff team is able to develop leading-edge practice which is specifically developed to meet the particular needs, or strengths, of the children on roll and the local community they come from. This practice might be linked to degree- or MA-level study and research projects. For example, when I was the deputy headteacher of an urban nursery centre, I noticed that Turkish-speaking children did not seem to be as engaged as other children in nursery activities. In the local area, outcomes for Turkish-speaking children later in their primary schooling were not as good as the outcomes for other children. So, I set up a series of focus groups to learn more about how Turkish-speaking parents understood early years education. This led to the development of a weekly group, with an interpreter, where we talked together about what the children were doing at home and in nursery, and, crucially, considered how this might link to their learning. Parents who had been unsure about how children learnt through play, because their own education had been more formal, saw how their children were learning in nursery and talked about the way they could help this further at home. The nursery learnt a lot about the children's home culture, play and learning, and was able to make changes to its approach and resourcing. For example, singing Turkish songs all together at group time helped the Turkish-speaking children to feel more of a sense of belonging. In turn, the outcomes for those children by the end of their time in nursery improved significantly.

Case study

An infant school was recently graded Requires Improvement for its early years. The headteacher felt that some new approaches were needed, and the EYFS co-ordinator had been very impressed by a conference she had attended on Natural Play. So, the school engaged the conference speaker to work with them as a consultant. She suggested that the school should develop a Forest School and that most of the tables should be removed from the classes, and replaced with small carpet areas with wicker baskets full of natural and open-ended resources. The consultant took the team to see an inspirational nursery and reception unit, where the children could move freely between the different classes and a beautiful garden with a huge sand and water area, and used a Forest School area every day.

Lots of new resources were bought and plans were drawn up to develop the outdoors. It took many months to develop the plans, cost them and arrange for the necessary tenders. The headteacher and the co-ordinator found themselves attending numerous meetings discussing materials, specifications and problems with drainage on the school site.

However, when an HMI (Her Majesty's Inspector) came to monitor progress, the EYFS was judged still to be a cause for concern. The HMI commented, in verbal feedback, that staff did not seem to have the skills to manage or develop the children's play, so that, when she observed, many of the areas were a chaotic mix of different materials which were sometimes just tipped out of the baskets by the children. There was no evidence that the children were making adequate progress in their learning.

The school used the Three Phase Model to reflect on its development, and realised that the best fit for where they currently were, was Phase one. But they had been trying to develop the leading-edge practice they had observed and been inspired by, as if they were in Phase three.

Many staff were not confident about basic skills in interacting with children and encouraging their play, so bringing in a new approach without adequate support and training at this stage had just made the reception classes chaotic. The co-ordinator put a halt to any further changes and worked intensively with staff. She checked each classteacher's planning thoroughly and required everyone to share at least ten observation-based assessments with her every week. This highlighted that some staff were not at all sure what learning was going on when children were playing. Teachers were not using all the assessment information to help them to plan, so much of the planning was not matched well to the children's level of learning or their interests. The co-ordinator realised that she had been distracted by 'big plans' and was not focussing on the day-to-day support and management of her team. When she talked to team members individually, she found that some were more confident when developing play with children in a more structured way, for example playing with Lego with a small group. So she considered that it would be better to build their skills in areas of confidence, and then begin slowly to introduce more natural and open-ended materials. She realised that some staff needed daily support and encouragement – they could

(Continued)

(Continued)

not be 'left to it' whilst she was in meetings or working on the plans for the outdoors. She discussed this with the headteacher, and they agreed to scale back the changes to the outdoors and just focus on developing a small area for a Forest School rather than change everything. Once they had agreed the basic outline for the plans, they delegated the meetings to the School Business Manager, who reported back to them on progress, and this freed up more of their time to undertake joint work supporting staff and monitoring practice.

After a strong focus for a term on the basics of planning, assessment and supporting play and communication, the reception classes became much more settled and children were happier and more purposeful. Assessment information showed that children were making strong progress, especially in their communication. The co-ordinator began to use the new, natural resources for blocks of time once the children were more settled, and these were successful in encouraging more creative play and more collaboration. Less-confident staff were given time to observe how the resources were being managed and how they were benefitting the children, and the co-ordinator decided that she would then develop this approach across the whole team the following year.

2

The basics

Making sure you meet the legal requirements

Every early years provider, from the smallest pre-school to the largest maintained school with hundreds of children on roll in the EYFS, needs to have a plan and the systems in place to ensure compliance with the Statutory Framework. Losing your focus on this priority is an easy mistake to make, and one which can lead to disaster. You need to make sure that you get this right, and that you are continuously reviewing your provision to make sure that everything is in place.

If you are not sure where you stand, then the pro formas in Tables 2.1–2.3 has been put together to help you assess your current level of compliance, and also to track your progress as you improve. Please note that this is a quick guide: you should always check the full Statutory Framework document (Department for Education, 2014), and you should look out for updates.

From time to time, there may be other requirements which you are required to meet. So, it is vital that you keep up to date with changes by regularly reading a publication like *Nursery World*, signing up for email alerts with the Foundation Years website, or joining a professional association like the National Association of Day Nurseries, PACEY (Professional Association for Childcare and Early Years) or Early Education.

Table 2.1   Pro forma for the Statutory Framework

Section 1: The learning and development requirements

Key issue	Securely in place	Mostly in place	Not yet in place
You can demonstrate that your learning environment, planning and assessment (your 'educational programme') cover all three Prime Areas and all four Specific Areas of the EYFS.			
You can demonstrate that your educational programme considers the individual needs and interests of each child on roll.			
You can demonstrate that you consider whether any individual child might have a special need or disability which requires specialist support.			
For children whose home language is not English, you can demonstrate that you take reasonable steps to provide opportunities for children to develop and use their home language in play and learning.			
You can demonstrate that for each area of learning, you plan purposeful play and a mix of adult-led and child-initiated activity.			
You can demonstrate that you reflect on the different ways that children learn (the 'Characteristics of Effective Learning'), and this is reflected in your practice.			
You can demonstrate that you are tracking children's progress and share the information with parents.			

↗ **For a downloadable version of this pro forma, please visit: https://study.sagepub.com/grenier**

Table 2.2

Section Two: Assessment

Key issue	Securely in place	Mostly in place	Not yet in place
If you have children on roll between the ages of two and three, you review their progress and provide parents with a short written report (the 'Progress Check at Age Two').			
The Progress Check focusses particularly on any areas where there is a concern that a child has a developmental delay and how you are intending to address any issues or concerns.			

↗ **For a downloadable version of this pro forma, please visit: https://study.sagepub.com/grenier**

Table 2.3

Section Three: The safeguarding and welfare requirements

Key issue	Securely in place	Mostly in place	Not yet in place
You have and you implement a policy and procedures to safeguard children. Your policy is in line with the guidance and procedures of the relevant Local Safeguarding Children Board (LSCB).			
Your policy clearly states: • Action to be taken if an allegation is made against a member of staff. • Policy on the use of mobile phones and cameras in the setting.			
You have a designated practitioner who takes lead responsibility for safeguarding, liaising with local statutory children's services and with the LCSB.			
The lead practitioner must provide support, advice and guidance to any staff on an ongoing basis, and on any specific safeguarding issue as required.			
The lead practitioner must attend a child protection course. (Full requirements are set out in Section 3.5)			
You must train all staff to: • Understand the safeguarding policy and procedures. • Have up to date knowledge of safeguarding issues. • Identify signs of potential abuse and neglect, and respond in a timely and appropriate way. (Full requirements are set out in Section 3.6)			
You must have regard to the statutory guidance *Working Together to Safeguard Children* (www.gov.uk/government/publications/working-together-to-safeguard-children–2) and notify agencies with statutory responsibilities without delay if you have concerns about children's safety or welfare.			
You must inform Ofsted of any allegations of serious harm or abuse by any person living, working or looking after children at the premises. You must notify Ofsted of the action taken in respect of the allegations at the latest within 14 days. (Full requirements are set out in Section 3.8)			
You must ensure that people looking after children are suitable to fulfil the requirements of their roles, and have effective systems in place to ensure that practitioners and anyone else having regular contact with the children (including those living or working on the premises) are suitable.			

(Continued)

Table 2.3 (Continued)

Key issue	Securely in place	Mostly in place	Not yet in place
You obtain Enhanced Criminal Records checks and Barred List checks for every person over the age of 16 who works directly with children, lives on the premises on which childcare is provided and/or works on the premises.			
You tell staff that they are expected to disclose any convictions, court orders, reprimands and warnings that may affect their suitability to work with children (whether before or during their employment at the setting).			
You do not allow anyone whose suitability has not been checked to have unsupervised contact with children.			
You check and record the following information about each member of staff: • Qualifications. • Identity. • Vetting – including the criminal records disclosure number, date disclosure was obtained and details of who obtained it.			
You meet your responsibilities under the Safeguarding Vulnerable Groups Act (2006), including the duty to make a referral to the Disclosure and Barring Service where a member of staff is dismissed (or would have been, had they not left the setting first) because they have harmed a child or put a child at risk of harm.			
You are aware of the regulations covering disqualification, detailed in Sections 3.14 to 3.18.			
You ensure that practitioners are not under the influence of alcohol or any other substance which may affect their ability to care for children.			
You ensure that any practitioner taking medication which may affect their ability to care for children: • Seeks medical advice. • Only works directly with the children if that advice confirms that the medication is unlikely to impair their ability to look after children properly.			
You ensure that staff medication is securely stored and out of the reach of children at all times.			
You ensure that all staff receive induction training to help them understand their roles and responsibilities, including: • Emergency evacuation procedures. • Safeguarding.			

Key issue	Securely in place	Mostly in place	Not yet in place
• Child protection. • Equality policy. • Health and safety issues.			
You ensure that all staff undertake appropriate training and use professional development opportunities to ensure that they offer quality learning and development experiences for children that continually improve.			
You have a supervision system in place for all staff who have contact with children and families, providing support, coaching and training for the practitioner and promoting the interests of children.			
The manager of the setting holds at least a full and relevant level 3 qualification and at least half of all other staff hold at least a full and relevant level 2 qualification. There is a named deputy who is capable and qualified to take charge in the manager's absence.			
At least one person who has a current paediatric first aid certificate must be on the premises and available at all times when children are present, and must accompany children on outings: • Paediatric first aid training must be relevant for workers caring for young children and, where relevant, babies. • The paediatric first aider must be able to respond to emergencies quickly, taking into account the number of children and staff, and the layout of the premises.			
You ensure that staff have sufficient understanding and use of English to ensure the wellbeing of children in their care, for example to: • Keep records in English. • Liaise with other agencies in English. • Summon emergency help in English. • Understand instructions in English, e.g. for safety of medicines or food hygiene.			
Each child is assigned a key person, in order to • Help ensure that every child's care is tailored to suit their individual needs. • Help the child become familiar with the setting. • Offer a settled relationship for the child. • Build a relationship with their parents.			
Your staffing arrangements meet the needs of all children and ensure their safety:			

(Continued)

Table 2.3 (Continued)

Key issue	Securely in place	Mostly in place	Not yet in place
• You ensure that children are adequately supervised and deploy staff to meet children's needs. • You inform parents about staff deployment and, where relevant and practical, aim to involve them in these decisions. • Children must *usually* be within sight *and* hearing of staff. • Children must *always* be within sight *or* hearing of staff.			
You calculate the staff:child ratio as follows: • You only include those aged 17 or over in ratios. • Staff under 17 are supervised at all times. • You can include students on long-term placements, volunteers (aged 17 and over) and staff working as apprentices in early education (aged 16 and over) as long as you are satisfied they are competent and responsible.			
You calculate the ratio and qualification requirements below in respect of staff available to work directly with children. If you supply overnight care, you apply the relevant ratios and ensure one member of staff is awake at all times.			
You meet or exceed the following minimum ratios and requirements. For children aged under two: • At least one member of staff for every three children. • At least one member of staff holds a full and relevant level 3 qualification and is suitably experienced in working with children under two. • At least half of all other staff hold a full and relevant level 2 qualification. • At least half of all staff must have received training that specifically addresses the care of babies. • Where there is an under-twos room, you judge that the member of staff in charge has suitable experience of working with under-twos. For children aged two: • At least one member of staff for every four children. • At least one member of staff holds a full and relevant level 3 qualification. • At least half of all other staff hold a full and relevant level 2 qualification.			

Key issue	Securely in place	Mostly in place	Not yet in place
For children aged three and over in registered early years provision where a person with Qualified Teacher Status, Early Years Professional Status, Early Years Teacher Status or another suitable level 6 qualification is working directly with the children: • At least one member of staff for every 13 children. • At least one member of staff must hold a full and relevant level 3 qualification.			
For children aged three and over in registered early years provision where there is *not* a person with Qualified Teacher Status, Early Years Professional Status, Early Years Teacher Status or another suitable level 6 qualification working directly with the children: • At least one member of staff for every eight children. • At least one member of staff must hold a full and relevant level 3 qualification. • At least half of all other staff must hold a full and relevant level 2 qualification.			
For children aged three and over in independent schools where there is a person with Qualified Teacher Status, Early Years Professional Status, Early Years Teacher Status or another suitable level 6 qualification, an instructor or another suitably qualified overseas-trained teacher working directly with the children: • For classes where the majority of children will reach the age of five or older within the school year, there must be at least one member of staff for every 30 children. • For all other classes there must be at least one member of staff for every 13 children. • At least one member of staff must hold a full and relevant level 3 qualification.			
For children aged three and over in registered early years independent schools where there is *not* a person with Qualified Teacher Status, Early Years Professional Status, Early Years Teacher Status or another suitable level 6 qualification, an instructor or another suitably qualified overseas-trained teacher working directly with the children: • At least one member of staff for every eight children. • At least one member of staff must hold a full and relevant level 3 qualification. • At least half of all other staff must hold a full and relevant level 2 qualification.			

(Continued)

Table 2.3 (Continued)

Key issue	Securely in place	Mostly in place	Not yet in place
For children aged three and over in maintained nursery schools and nursery classes in maintained schools: • At least one member of staff for every 13 children. • At least one member of staff must be a school teacher as defined by Section 122 of the Education Act (2002). • At least one other member of staff must hold a full and relevant level 3 qualification.			
If you are responsible for a reception class in a maintained school: • You adhere to the Infant Class Size Regulations (2012) which limit the size of infant classes to 30 pupils per school teacher while an ordinary teaching session is conducted. • You do not count teaching assistants, higher level teaching assistants or other support staff as 'school teachers'. (For full details see Section 3.38)			
If you are responsible for a reception class which is mixed with younger children, you determine ratios within mixed groups, guided by the relevant ratio requirements and the needs of individual children in the group. In exercising that discretion you meet the statutory requirements relating to infant class size.			
If you are in a school with partner providers, you ensure that they meet the relevant ratio requirements for their provision.			
If you manage before or after school care or holiday provision for children who normally attend reception class (or older) during the day: • You ensure that there are sufficient staff as for a class of 30 children. • You must determine how many staff are needed to ensure the safety and welfare of the children, bearing in mind the types of activity and the age and needs of the children. • You must determine what qualifications, if any, the manager and/or staff should have. • You do *not* need to meet the learning and development requirements of the EYFS. • You should ensure that practitioners discuss with parents/carers and school staff/teachers the support that will be offered to the children.			

Key issue	Securely in place	Mostly in place	Not yet in place
You must promote the good health of children attending the setting and have a procedure, discussed with parents, for responding to children who are ill or infectious. You must take necessary steps to prevent the spread of infection and take appropriate action if children are ill.			
You must have and implement and policy and procedures for administering medicines which includes systems for: • Obtaining information about a child's needs for medicines. • Keeping this information up to date. • Training staff where administering the medicine requires medical or technical knowledge.			
You ensure that: • Medicines are not usually administered unless they have been prescribed for a child by a doctor, dentist, nurse or pharmacist. • Medicines containing aspirin are only given if prescribed by a doctor. • Medicine (both prescription and non-prescription) is only administered where written permission for that particular medicine has been obtained from the child's parent/carer. • A written record is kept each time a medicine is administered to a child and you inform the parent/carer on the same day or as soon as reasonably practicable.			
You ensure that any meals, snacks and drinks provided are healthy, balanced and nutritious, and: • You obtain information about any special dietary requirements, preferences and food allergies the child has, and any special health requirements. • You ensure that fresh drinking water is available and accessible at all times. • You ensure that you record and act on information from parents/carers about a child's dietary needs.			
You ensure that there is an area which is adequately equipped to provide healthy meals, snacks and drinks for children as necessary, and that: • You have suitable facilities for the hygienic preparation of food for children, if necessary including suitable sterilisation equipment for babies' food. • All staff involved in preparing and handling food receive training in food hygiene.			

(Continued)

Table 2.3 (Continued)

Key issue	Securely in place	Mostly in place	Not yet in place
You ensure that there is a first aid box accessible at all times with appropriate content for use with children, and: • You keep a written record of accidents or injuries and first aid treatment. • Parents/carers are informed of any accident or injury sustained by the child and of any first aid treatment given on the same day, or as soon as reasonably practicable.			
You must notify Ofsted of any serious accident, illness or injury to, or death of any child while in your care, and of the action taken: • Notification must be made as soon as is reasonably practicable, but in any event within 14 days of the incident occurring. • You must notify local child protection agencies of any serious accident or injury to, or death of, a child in your care and you must act on any advice from those agencies.			
You are aware of your responsibility to manage children's behaviour in an appropriate way: • You take all reasonable steps to ensure that corporal punishment is not given by any person who cares for, works in or lives in the premises. • You ensure that corporal punishment is not threatened, and no other punishment is used or threatened which could adversely affect a child's wellbeing.			
Physical intervention may be used: • To avert immediate danger to any person (including the child). • Or to manage the child's behaviour if absolutely necessary. You must keep a record of any occasion where physical intervention is used, and you must inform parents/carers on the same day or as soon as reasonably practicable.			
You ensure that: • Your premises, including overall floor space and outdoor spaces, are fit for purpose for the age of the children and the activities provided on the premises. • You comply with requirements of health and safety legislation (including fire safety and hygiene requirements).			

Key issue	Securely in place	Mostly in place	Not yet in place
You must: • Take reasonable steps to ensure the safety of children, staff and others on the premises in the case of fire or any other emergency. • Have an emergency evacuation procedure. • Have appropriate fire detection and control equipment which is in working order. • Have fire exits which are clearly identifiable and fire doors which are free of obstruction and easily opened from the inside.			
You do not allow smoking in or on the premises when children are present or about to be present.			
You organise premises and equipment in a way that meets the needs of children. You meet the following indoor space requirements: • Children under two: 3.5 m² per child. • Two-year-olds: 2.5 m² per child. • Children aged three to five years: 2.3 m² per child.			
You provide access to an outdoor play area or, if that is not possible, ensure that outdoor activities are planned and taken on a daily basis (unless circumstances make this inappropriate, for example unsafe weather conditions).			
You follow the legal responsibilities under the Equality Act (2010) (for example, the provisions on reasonable adjustments).			
You ensure that sleeping children are frequently checked.			
If you care for children under the age of two, you ensure that there is a separate baby room for them; however, you ensure that children in a baby room have contact with older children and are moved into the older age group when appropriate.			
In respect to hygiene facilities, you ensure that: • There are an adequate number of toilets and hand basins available; there should usually be separate toilet facilities for adults. • There are suitable hygienic changing facilities for changing any children who are in nappies. • An adequate supply of clean bedding, towels, spare clothes and any other necessary items is always available.			
You ensure that there is an area where staff may talk to parents/carers confidentially. There is an area for staff to take breaks away from areas being used by children.			

(Continued)

Table 2.3 (Continued)

Key issue	Securely in place	Mostly in place	Not yet in place
In order to ensure children's safety: • You only release children into the care of individuals who have been notified to you by the parent and you ensure that children do not leave the premises unsupervised. • You take all reasonable steps to prevent unauthorised persons entering the premises and you have an agreed procedure for checking the identity of visitors. • If you keep children overnight, you must consider what additional measures are necessary.			
You have public liability insurance.			
You take all reasonable steps to ensure staff and children in your care are not exposed to risks and you are able to demonstrate how you are managing risks: • You determine whether it is helpful to make some written risk assessments in relation to specific issues, to inform staff practice, and to demonstrate how you are managing risks if asked by parents/carers or inspectors. • Risk assessments should identify aspects of the environment that need to be checked on a regular basis, when and by whom those aspects will be checked, and how the risk will be removed or minimised.			
You keep children safe when on outings: • You assess the risks or hazards which may arise for the children. • You identify the steps to be taken to remove, minimise and manage those risks and hazards. • Your risk assessment must include consideration of adult:child ratios. The risk assessment does not necessarily need to be in writing, this is for you to judge.			
Vehicles in which children are being transported, and the drivers of those vehicles, must be adequately insured.			
You have arrangements in place to support children with special educational needs or disabilities (SEND): • Maintained nursery schools and other providers who are funded by the local authority must have regard to the SEND Code of Practice. • Maintained nursery schools must identify a member of staff to act as Special Educational Needs Co-ordinator (SENCO) and other providers are expected to identify a SENCO.			

Key issue	Securely in place	Mostly in place	Not yet in place
You must maintain records and obtain and share information (with parents/carers, other professionals working with the child, the police, social services and Ofsted) to: • Ensure the safe and efficient management of the setting. • Help ensure that the needs of all children are met. You must: • Enable a two-way flow of information with parents/carers and between providers if the child attends more than one setting. • Incorporate parents'/carers' comments into children's records, if requested.			
You ensure that records are easily accessible and available. Confidential information and records about staff and children are held securely and only accessible and available to those who have a right or professional need to see them. You are aware of your responsibilities under the Data Protection Act (1998) and the Freedom of Information Act (2000).			
You make sure that all staff understand the need to protect the privacy of children in their care and are aware of the legal requirements to handle information relating to the child in a way that ensures confidentiality.			
You ensure that parents/carers are given access to all records about their child.			
You retain records relating to individual children for a reasonable period of time after they have left the provision.			
You record the following information about each child in your care: • Full name. • Date of birth. • Name and address of every parent/carer known to you. • Information about any other person who has parental responsibility for the child. • Which parent(s)/carer(s) the child normally lives with. • Emergency contact details for parents/carers.			
You must make the following information available to parents/carers: • How the EYFS is being delivered in the setting, and how parents and/or carers can access more information.			

(Continued)

Table 2.3 (Continued)

Key issue	Securely in place	Mostly in place	Not yet in place
• The range and type of activities and experiences provided for children, the daily routines of the setting, and how parents and carers can share learning at home. • How the setting supports children with special educational needs and disabilities. • Food and drinks provided for children. • Details of the provider's policies and procedures including the procedure to be followed in the event of a parent and/or carer failing to collect a child at the appointed time, or in the event of a child going missing at, or away from, the setting. • Staffing in the setting. • The name of their child's key person and their role. • A telephone number for parents and/or carers to contact in an emergency.			
You have a written procedure for dealing with concerns and complaints from parents/carers: • You keep a written record of any complaints and their outcomes. • You investigate written complaints relating to your fulfilment of EYFS requirements and notify complainants of the outcome of the investigation within 28 days of receiving the complaints. • You must make the record of complaints available to Ofsted on request.			
You make available to parents/carers details about how to contact Ofsted if they believe you are not meeting the EYFS requirements. You notify parents/carers if you become aware that you are to be inspected by Ofsted and you supply a copy of the report to parents/carers.			
You must hold the following information: • Name, home address and telephone number of the provider and any other person living or employed on the premises. • Name, home address and telephone number of anyone else who will regularly be in unsupervised contact with the children attending the early years provision. • A daily record of the names of the children being cared for on the premises, their hours of attendance and the names of each child's key person. • Your certificate of registration (which must be displayed at the setting and shown to parents and/or carers on request).			

Key issue	Securely in place	Mostly in place	Not yet in place
You make sure that you notify Ofsted of any change: • In the address of the premises. • To the premises which may affect the space available to children and the quality of childcare available to them. • In the name or address of the provider, or the provider's other contact information. • To the person who is managing the early years provision.			
You make sure you notify Ofsted of: • Any proposal to change the hours during which childcare is provided; or to provide overnight care. • Any significant event which is likely to affect the suitability of the early years provider or any person who cares for, or is in regular contact with, children on the premises to look after children. • Where the early years provision is provided by a company, any change in the name or registration number of the company. • Where the early years provision is provided by a charity, any change in the name or registration number of the charity. • Where the childcare is provided by a partnership, body corporate or unincorporated association, any change to the 'nominated individual'. Where the childcare is provided by a partnership, body corporate or unincorporated association whose sole or main purpose is the provision of childcare, any change to the individuals who are partners in, or a director, secretary or other officer or member of its governing body.			
You ensure that Ofsted are notified if there is a change of manager. Where it is reasonably practicable to do so, notification must be made in advance. In other cases, notification must be made as soon as is reasonably practicable, but always within 14 days.			
Where providers are required to notify Ofsted about a change of person involved in the management of the setting (e.g. on a management board or where the school governing body is the 'registered person') you must give Ofsted the new person's name, any former names or aliases, date of birth, and home address. (For full details see Section 3.78)			

For a downloadable version of this pro forma, please visit: https://study.sagepub.com/grenier

3

Building staff skills, professionalism and morale to create and sustain effective EYFS practice

The recruitment and retention of skilled and effective staff members is one of the biggest challenges for any setting. The NNEB (Nursery Nurse Examination Board) diploma was scrapped in the mid-1990s. With its prioritisation of child development, observation and on-the-job assessment, it was considered a 'gold standard' and there have been concerns ever since about standards and consistency in level 3 qualifications. The government-sponsored Nutbrown Review (2012) reported that: 'many level 3 qualifications currently on offer are insufficient in content and standard'.

Recruiting effective qualified teachers to work in the EYFS can be equally challenging. Many teacher training courses have a very limited focus on the EYFS and hardly cover topics such as play, learning outdoors or the key person approach at all. The development of the Early Years Teacher Status has confused matters significantly, because Early Years Teachers (EYTs) do not have full qualified teacher status and cannot therefore be appointed to teach reception or nursery classes in maintained schools. They can be appointed to academies and free schools, because there is no requirement for these schools to appoint qualified teachers to any position.

A significant number of early years practitioners have completed degrees, mostly in Early Childhood Studies or Foundation Degrees in Education. Some of them are highly experienced staff who have completed a reputable degree which deepens their existing experience and practical skills and knowledge. Unfortunately, it is also the case that a large number have received poor tuition in large groups of 30 students or more, and have gained a degree without much specialist knowledge of teaching and learning in the early years.

So, it is no wonder that Professor Iram Siraj (2010: 20) has complained of England's 'muddle in training, with an ever-more diverse workforce'. In effect, what this means is that leadership of the EYFS requires a substantial focus on supporting and developing your team. Many well-qualified staff will need a significant amount of on-the-job training in order to develop their effectiveness: you cannot rely on their qualifications or make any assumptions about the quality of the training.

On the other hand, the large majority of EYFS staff are very committed to their work and to the children. In the days when local authorities ran comprehensive training and development programmes, it was always staff in the EYFS who accessed the most courses. So, as long as you can motivate and support your practitioners, you have a very good chance of building a strong and effective team.

Developing your staff team: Basic requirements

Before you start to work in a sustained way to support and develop the members of your team, you will need to have a set of basic policies outlining your approach which have been agreed with your governors or management board, and which have been shared with staff. It is essential that these policies are consistent with the law in respect of employment, equalities and all other relevant areas. They also need to be compliant with the EYFS Statutory Framework and with Ofsted (as regulator and/or inspection agency). If you are an early years setting, you may wish to adopt or develop policies from the National Association of Day Nurseries (NDNA), Pre-School Learning Alliance (PLA) or another reputable professional organisation. If you are a school, you may wish to adopt model policies from your Human Resources or Personnel Department. To carry out the work outlined in the rest of this chapter, you will need first to have policies covering the following areas at least:

- Recruitment.
- Induction.
- Probation.
- Performance Management or Appraisal.
- Capability.

Assessing the strengths and skills within your team

It is essential that you have a systematic approach to this, and that you keep thorough records of your work so that you can demonstrate that individuals and teams are improving over time. You should make sure that all staff understand your approach and ensure that you have an agreed Appraisal or Performance Management Policy.

You will be assessing the strengths and needs of every member of staff from your first engagement with them, at interview. This will need to be followed up during the induction period, and then move into an annual review cycle. You will also need to consider how well the staff work together as a team, again considering strengths and weaknesses.

Appointment

When you appoint a new member of staff, make a quick and focussed note about their strengths during the selection process, and any areas which might need development. You could use or adapt the pro forma given in Table 3.1 for this.

Table 3.1

Name of new member of staff	
Date appointed	
Briefly note any strengths and any areas for development arising from the following aspects of the selection process:	
1. Observation of their practice with the children.	
2. Reference.	
3. Written statement/application form.	
4. Answers to interview questions.	
Any other notes or comments	

↗ **For a downloadable version of this pro forma, please visit: https://study.sagepub.com/grenier**

This form can be shared with the member of staff on their first day with you, and it would be good practice to allow them to add their own comments.

During induction training, you will need to ensure that the key points from the pro forma are addressed as fully as possible. You may need to draw particular attention to elements of your standard induction, or you may need to tailor parts of the process to the individual.

It is also advisable to have a code of conduct, drawn up in consultation with the whole team. If you ask each person to sign the code of conduct when they start work, it is more likely to be read carefully and followed.

Induction training

Offering a proper induction to new staff, and a rapid induction to agency staff, is perhaps one of the most neglected areas of practice in the early years. We end up neglecting induction, I would argue, for one simple reason: everyone is so pushed for time. But there is a strong case to make that this is not an efficient time-saver: staff who have not been properly inducted will work less confidently, take longer to settle into the team, and may get important things wrong. The following suggestions may help you to design an effective process.

Rapid induction

This should be suitable for agency staff, students on placement, and as the first introduction to working in the team for a new member of staff. It will need to cover the absolute basics quickly and clearly. You might want to include space on the form for the new member of staff or student. It is good practice for the person being inducted, and for the person offering the induction, to sign the form at the end so that you have a formal record that induction took place. It can be helpful to allow a short period of time after the induction session has finished for the person to go through the form and check in case they have any further questions, or in case anything is unclear.

The pro forma given in Table 3.2 may be helpful for you to use or adapt.

Table 3.2

Name of member of staff being inducted	
Name of member of staff leading the induction session	
Date	
Overview: your team and the areas where you will be working.	Your notes
Names of your team leader and the senior leadership team.	
Health and safety: fire and evacuation procedures, first aid, accident book and what to do if you are concerned something isn't safe.	
Child protection and safeguarding procedures, and what to do if you are concerned about a child.	
Our approach to the early years: managing children's behaviour, managing the learning environment, play	

(Continued)

Table 3.2 (Continued)

and interaction, key person and relationships with parents.	
Equalities and inclusion: our approach and key information about specific children.	
Professional conduct: confidentiality, promoting equality and challenging prejudice, acceptable use of ICT and our no-mobile policy.	
Basic procedures for staff working here: start/end times, breaks, signing in and out, lockers, and what to do if you are sick or cannot attend work.	

What you can expect from us: We will do everything we can to ensure you have a positive experience of working here. We will treat you with politeness and respect. We will help you to learn and develop. We will ensure the working environment is safe and healthy, and we will make any reasonable changes to the building or equipment to meet your needs. We will support you to be the best you can be.

What we expect from you: That you will always focus on the children and their families as your first priority. You will show engagement and enthusiasm in your play with the children, indoors and outside. You will work positively with all team members and promote our inclusion and equalities policies. You will always follow our procedures and raise any concerns you might have about a child's safety or wellbeing.

*Please review your notes: If there is anything you are not sure about, please feel confident to ask **before** you start work with the children. As a 'fresh pair of eyes' you may notice possible hazards and other problems: please tell us if this is the case.*

 For a downloadable version of this pro forma, please visit: https://study.sagepub.com/grenier

Full induction and probation process

Your full induction process should cover all the key areas of practice, procedures and policies. It should link to the probation period, so that you are clear about how you train and support each new member of staff to work according to your ethos, policies and approaches, and ensure that they reach an acceptable level of performance before they are confirmed in their post.

Normally, a probation period will be around three months. You do not want to offer a permanent position to a member of staff if you have reservations about their skills or their ability to work with others and uphold your core principles. If a new member of staff does not meet the required standards, then – as set out in your policy – you may either extend their probationary period or dismiss them. However hard this type of management approach feels, it is essential to be strong and professional. Your children deserve practitioners who can provide them with an appropriate experience of early education and care: they will not get another chance. Likewise, your team members need to be able to rely on each other and cannot be expected to 'carry' an inadequate colleague.

The pro forma given in Table 3.3 suggests one approach to induction and probation.

Table 3.3

Name of member of staff being inducted	
Name of mentor	
Name of team leader	
Date	

Induction	
Session One: Our ethos, vision and ways of working (two hours).	Sign when completed.
Session Two: Safeguarding (half day).	
Session Three: Learning through play and managing the learning environment (half day).	
Session Four: Key person approach, inclusion and behaviour management (half day).	
Session Five: Partnership with parents (two hours).	

Probation

If anyone has concerns at any point during probation, these should be referred to the headteacher or deputy ASAP.

End of first week: Your comments.	
End of first week: Your team leader's comments.	
End of first month: Your comments.	
End of first month: Your team leader's comments.	
End of probation period: Your comments.	
End of probation period: Your team leader's comments.	

Team leader's recommendation:

- Pass probation now
- Extend probation by another .... (weeks) to observe improved performance in the following areas (maximum of two):

  1.

  2.

(Continued)

Table 3.3 (Continued)

• Fail probation (N.B. this can only be selected if concerns about performance have already been referred to the headteacher/deputy and an action plan for support has been in place).
Any further comments from your team leader. Your comments.
Targets (identify support and training opportunities, too) in place until the start of the annual performance management cycle (maximum of two): 1.   2.

 For a downloadable version of this pro forma, please visit: https://study.sagepub.com/grenier

Annual review

All staff should have an annual appraisal or performance management cycle. This should be a collaborative process: it allows you as the manager to make and share an assessment of the member of staff's capability, and it allows the member of staff to self-evaluate their own effectiveness and to put forward suggestions for their continuing professional development, highlight any difficulties they may be experiencing, and ask for support if needed. The more the process feels like something that is 'done with' staff rather than 'done to' them, the more useful it is likely to be.

You will also want to keep a careful balance between tailoring the process to each member of staff individually, and ensuring that the team develop together. If, for example, you identified three targets with associated training for every member of staff, with a team of 20, you, as the manager, would be left monitoring as many as 60 targets and have to organise as many as 60 training sessions. Your staff will all be following individual pathways and this might make it hard to make sure they develop consistently in key areas.

The annual review process should be based on practice and on professional dialogue, and not be an onerous, form-filling exercise. The starting point could be an observation of the member of staff's work with the children, followed by a discussion which could be structured and recorded by the pro forma given in Table 3.4.

What should you do if you are concerned about the capability of a member of the team?

This is certainly one of the most difficult aspects of the job, as well as one of the most important. If you have 'niggles' or a gut feeling that a member of the team

Table 3.4

Name of member of staff	
Review of last year's targets or summary of probation targets	
Self-evaluation by member of staff (prompts): • What went well this year? • Have you experienced any difficulties? • Which areas of the provision do you think are going especially well? • Which areas need review and improvement? • Are there any colleagues or any children who you are concerned about?	
Observation of practice: Key strengths and key areas for development.	
Three targets for development in the year ahead. • At least one target should link to the improvement plan as part of whole-staff development. • Ensure targets are SMART (Specific, Measurable, Achievable, Realistic, Time-limited). • Set six-monthly interim review date. • Professional development opportunities linked to targets (N.B. these will usually consist of observing or working with a colleague to develop practice).	1. 2. 3.
Any other notes or comments.	

For a downloadable version of this pro forma, please visit: https://study.sagepub.com/grenier

is not working effectively, there are several steps it is important to take immediately. Sticking your head in the sand and hoping things will get better of their own accord is a natural human instinct, but one that will not help this situation at all. On the other hand, most of us have experienced a time when a sharp focus on our performance at work has caused us to feel anxious and to start doubting our abilities. This is quite likely to have a sharply negative effect on the quality of our work. In the early years, teams are usually small and people work quite intensively together – so, unsettling one member of the team can adversely affect everyone else, too. Staff are unlikely to be able to care for others – for children and their parents – if they themselves feel uncared for.

Even more worrying is the danger that what starts as addressing a concern about performance turns into workplace bullying. Perhaps because of the emotional pressures of looking after others, it is sadly the case that bullying and unprofessional behaviour appear to be very common in the 'caring professions'. For example, the UK National Workplace Bullying Advice line reported in 2004 that staff from education, healthcare and social care were the most likely to contact them about being bullied (Bullyonline, 2004) and more recent reports have claimed that workplace bullying is rife in education and health-care. Indeed, David Prior, chair of the Care Quality Commission, noted in 2014 that (*The Telegraph*, 2014) many hospitals had a 'toxic' bullying culture that 'stigmatises and ostracises those who raise concerns or complaints'. In my experience, much the same could be said of some schools and early years settings. So, before taking any action, always check yourself and make sure you are being fair, not adding unnecessary pressure to a situation, or bullying someone. If in doubt ask a trustworthy colleague for their opinion.

Those notes of caution should not be read as an excuse to do nothing, however. You, your team and the provision exist for one reason alone: to make a difference to the lives of the children you are responsible for. It is very often the case that when an early years setting or a school goes into decline, it is because there is a preoccupation with the dynamics between the staff, rather than a focus on the primary task at hand. As the leader or manager of the team, you cannot duck your responsibility to address issues of performance or professional conduct; and if the difficulties are too great for you to solve, then you need to ask for help. Problems with performance will not go away of their own accord.

These are some of the steps you might take if you are worried about the performance of a member of staff:

- Firstly, check that expectations and procedures have been clearly set out, and understood. You cannot focus on a single individual's poor performance if you have not made your standards clear. Consider whether some general support or advice to the whole team might be appropriate.

- Secondly, consider whether peer support might be effective. Many early years practitioners pride themselves - rightly - on the way that they get on with the job, muck in, and do not draw attention to themselves as individuals. But, as managers and leaders, we also need to promote a culture in which we can acknowledge publicly that some individuals are particularly good at what they do. This is not the same as favouritism, which involves treating some individuals better than others.

Case study

When Rabia, the nursery manager, spent the morning reviewing the quality of 'Rainbow Room' for two-year-olds, she noticed that there were problems at the end of the session when there was 'key group time'. Each key person gathered their four key children onto a small mat in their special area in the room. Fatima, the room leader, gently encouraged her children to come together. One of them, who was new to the nursery, did not want to come and sit down, so she was left playing contentedly with the jigsaws at the nearby table. However, Chloe, one of the newer members of staff, was struggling to engage the children in her group. She began to sing a song but then gave up after a few moments because the children did not join in. Then she reached into the book box and picked out a book which turned out to be too difficult for many of the children in her group to understand. One of the children started to get up in order to move away, so Chloe pulled him onto her lap and he struggled there, wanting to get away. Fatima then quietly brought her children over and sang songs with both groups.

When the manager met with Fatima to give feedback, she commented on how good her practice was. Fatima said that she was frustrated by Chloe's poor practice and found that she kept on having to take over from her.

When they discussed this difficult situation in more depth, it became clear that Chloe had strengths in playing with the children. But if she set up an adult-guided activity, she would often be very controlling so the children would move away. Her key group time was invariably poor and some children were 'voting with their feet' and coming to Fatima instead.

Although the nursery had a policy of keeping group sizes small, the manager judged that it would be better to combine Fatima and Chloe's groups for a few weeks. She suggested that, for a week, Fatima should lead the group times and ask Chloe to observe her practice. Fatima should check that Chloe was noticing key aspects of her practice, like how she managed the children, encouraged them to engage, and how she chose appropriate books and songs and kept the group time short (just five minutes) and varied, as was appropriate for the children's age. During the next week, Chloe started the group time off with a song, sometimes with movement and dancing. Fatima wanted Chloe to copy her approach at first. Gradually, Chloe improved and after a fortnight she was managing the whole five minutes well. The manager supported and encouraged both members of staff throughout. At the end, during a supervision session, she encouraged Fatima to think about how she had become frustrated with Chloe and just expected her to get better without any support. Fatima reflected that sometimes she expected everyone in her team to work to the same standard as her, without necessarily modelling good practice or spending time mentoring.

If you are sure that enough support has been offered, then it is important to move into a more structured approach. Although it is not easy to have this type of conversation with a member of staff, it is often something of a relief for both parties if problems can be aired in a respectful and professional way. You will need to arrange a time and a suitable, confidential place for the meeting, and make sure you will not be interrupted or distracted by phone calls or other communications. It is better to set a fairly short timescale for this type of meeting – about 15 to 20 minutes.

Explain that you have some concerns and you wish to raise these informally, in the spirit of problem-solving. Briefly and clearly state what your concerns are, and ask the member of staff if they recognise them. You may wish also to ask if there is anything which might be getting in the way of the member of staff doing their job as well as possible, and give a general opportunity to the member of staff to talk about how things are going. But do not allow the meeting to be derailed from discussing your concerns, unless something which is clearly more urgent and important emerges (e.g. a member of staff complains about being discriminated against, in which case you will need to stop your meeting there and arrange a proper time to explore the problem in depth and you will need to consult with your personnel or human resources team first).

Otherwise, listen attentively and then summarise what the member of staff has said, and suggest how you will come back to those issues in due course. If important personal issues emerge, you might suggest that the member of staff seeks a referral for counselling through their GP. Or you could make a referral to Occupational Health, if applicable. But you must make sure to return to your key issue for the final few minutes of the discussion. Check that the member of staff is clear about your concerns. Find out if they have a suggestion for support or professional development. Say how you can help. End the meeting by setting a date a few weeks later, where you will be reviewing the matter, and remind the member of staff that this has been an informal meeting to explore a possible problem and to work together to solve it.

When you come to the review meeting, you will need to decide whether this informal approach is working well enough, and is therefore the appropriate way forward. If you judge that you need to use the formal procedures in your performance management policy, then talk to your personnel or human resources team first, and make sure that you are clear about the procedure. If you are in a very small setting, then you would be well-advised to seek professional support before you take any further action: you do not want to end up facing an employment tribunal, with all the associated costs and stress, because you acted without proper advice.

Your training and professional development programme

Systematic approaches to staff training and professional development are an essential part of your commitment to improving quality. Firstly, you must meet the statutory requirements around training in the areas of safeguarding and first aid, and ensure that you keep accurate records of the training undertaken by members of staff.

The statutory requirements in terms of qualifications should be seen as a minimum standard. So, although you can operate legally with a manager at level 3, and half your staff at level 2 with the other half unqualified, this is a team structure which is unlikely to ensure good-quality provision or good outcomes for the children. If your team is relatively poorly qualified, then the first steps you should take are to change this. The research evidence suggests that teams led by a qualified teacher or graduate-level practitioner are more effective, so this should be an early priority. Likewise, a realistic training strategy will be needed to ensure that your unqualified practitioners achieve a level 2 qualification, and to move your level 2s onto a level 3. But I would urge you to choose your training provider with care. Check that assessors will give each level 2 or level 3 candidate enough time, and that they will be rigorous about ensuring the standards are met. You may need to work together with other settings and schools to get the quality you need.

When it comes to your annual training programme, you will need to strike the right balance between individuals' professional development, and the need for the whole team to develop together. Schools have the fortunate advantage of five full days of training per year, though if you are leading a school-based EYFS team you may have to negotiate to ensure that your team's needs are not neglected as you sit through whole days of training which are focussed on the learning of the older children. If you are not a school, it is still important to close for whole-staff training days. This will involve negotiation, and there is no doubt that it will be inconvenient to working parents: in my experience, it is advisable to state clearly in your waiting list and admissions forms that you close for training. Explain that this is essential for the development of quality provision, and ask parents to support this.

Your whole-team days are very precious. Each training day should be very carefully aligned with your annual self-evaluation and improvement plan. Make sure that the trainer knows how you currently rate the area of practice and exactly what improvements you desire to make. If possible, plan for the trainer to visit before the day to observe practice with you, and to visit three or four weeks after the day to help you to evaluate whether you are making a good start with implementation. You can find high-quality trainers through national organisations like Early Education (www.early-education.org.uk), or you could ask colleagues for a recommendation. You may be able to reduce your costs by joining with another school or setting.

Your approach to the professional development of individual members of staff needs to be equally rigorous. Even with a small team of six, if you identify three areas for further training for each person you might find yourself trying to book 18 courses and to make complex cover arrangements that will take up an immense amount of your time. Even when you have done all that, you will still need to plan time for the staff to feedback and implement their training, and you will also need to monitor its impact. In any case, it is generally very difficult for an individual who goes on a training course to feed back what they have learnt in a meaningful way to the whole team, so you probably will not see any wider impact. Booking staff onto lots of courses is an approach to professional development which will cost you a great deal in time and money, for little return.

Instead, consider drawing up a concise annual development plan for each member of staff with two or three areas linked to whole-staff training, and clearly show how this is intended to contribute to your improvement plan. Occasionally, it may be right to identify some training opportunities which are individual to a member of staff, for example something related to the area which they lead on. But, as a rule, you can focus training on in-team opportunities, like time to observe the effective practice of another member of the team, with debriefing time to reflect on the different aspects of that practice and think about how to implement them. If you are planning to send staff out to attend courses, you may find it is better to choose a sequenced course with tasks to complete between sessions (e.g. three mornings on improving early communication, spread out over a month) so that you can be sure that the learning is making an impact on practice. Linking with a national organisation like Early Education or a local consortium like a Teaching School Alliance will mean that you can be sure of the ethos and quality of the training.

Table 3.5

Priority One Whole-team: Improve the assessment of children's communication.	Link to the development plan Better early identification and help for children at risk of delay in their communication.	Training and development Whole team: Three sessions based on Every Child a Talker. Individualised support: Fatima to support Chloe in assessing the communication of two of her key children and to check the assessments of the other six for accuracy.
Priority Two Whole-team: Improve parent involvement in children's learning.	Link to the development plan Parents say they receive helpful information about their child's development (Ofsted action).	Training and development Whole team: One session on promoting dialogue with parents during home visits. One session on developing parental involvement in Special Books. One day of joint training with three other settings, led by an Early Education Associate: Involving Parents as Partners.
Priority Three Individual: Develop skills and confidence for short key group times at the end of sessions.		Training and development Individual support and mentoring with Fatima. Observe Fatima's key groups; practise songs and reading engaging picture books on your own; gradually take over leading the group time with regular observation and feedback from Fatima.

Table 3.5 gives an example of the annual training plan for Chloe, the practitioner working with two-year-olds in the private nursery who was struggling with key group time.

Supervision

One of the statutory requirements which is often neglected, is that every early years setting must offer regular supervision to its staff. There is a great deal of confusion about the difference between managing people, supervising them, and offering them coaching. The reason for this confusion is probably twofold: firstly, all of those activities overlap a great deal, and secondly, the practice of supervision in early years settings was very underdeveloped when it was recommended in the 2011 Tickell Review. This meant that Dame Clare Tickell was not able to cite any examples of effective practice in her report.

Supervision is about providing staff with a space in which they can reflect on their work and raise issues of concern (for example, about individual children) – without supervision, there may be no time or no opportunity for this. Supervision can be managed in different ways: it can be offered individually to staff, or in pairs or groups, and it can be facilitated by members of the team, or by an outside member of staff. All of those decisions will depend on your determination of what is best for your context, and what is practically achievable. If you are going to use an outside member of staff, then you will need to check that the person you select is a trained and reputable counsellor (for example, they are on the BACP Register for Counsellors and Psychotherapists). If your team members are going to run supervision sessions themselves, then you will need to consider appropriate training and arrangements for oversight.

Table 3.6

Staff supervision
Names of participants
Time and date of meeting
Supervision should provide opportunities for staff to: • discuss any issues – particularly concerning children's development or well-being; • identify solutions to address issues as they arise; and • receive coaching to improve their personal effectiveness. (DfE, EYFS Statutory Framework, 2014) Prompts: • What's going well? • Let's look back at the last session and the agreed actions together. • What have you been thinking about, that it would be helpful to talk over? • Have you got any current concerns in your work?
Notes: Agreed actions following supervision (up to three): 1. 2. 3. Signed If there is any disagreement about this note or the actions please record your views below. As a member of staff you are required to sign the form to confirm that the session went ahead.

For a downloadable version of this pro forma, please visit: https://study.sagepub.com/grenier   ↖

Before making your decision about how to proceed, it may be useful to bear in mind why supervision became recommended practice. There are two principal reasons.

Firstly, researchers like Peter Elfer (2015) have suggested that supervision helps staff to become emotionally attuned to the children they are caring for, and underpins an effective key person approach. Without supervision, Elfer argues, staff can become over-focussed on routines (writing up observations, tidying up, keeping to the timetable) at the expense of their primary task of being aware of, and responding to, the individual needs of the children.

Secondly, a number of Serious Case Reviews (investigations following deaths and serious incidents) focussed on nurseries found that a contributing factor to the abuse of the child, was that staff had no forum for raising or exploring concerns. Staff may have experienced a 'gut feeling' that all was not well with a child, but were unable to say exactly what their concern was. However, they had been able to explore their concern through supervision, maybe they would have been able to put their concern into words and to report it. Similarly, staff may have been worried by a colleague's behaviour, but been unsure who to tell, or what to say.

You may find the pro forma given in Table 3.6 helpful for recording supervision sessions, or as a starting point to develop your own.

Developing your aims and objectives with your team

This is a process which is best kept relatively simple, and best achieved using straightforward language. I think that the process which is suggested by the Results Based Accountability (http://resultsaccountability.com) method is a practical way to begin: arguably, you want something that is expressed in a straightforward way and helps you to work together, rather than something that is rousing and poetic, takes months to write and gets relegated to the back of everyone's minds as soon as it is finished. If you are interested, it will be worth your while to explore this approach in more depth, otherwise for the limited task of developing your aims and objectives, you might wish to use the following method.

Your aims could be a high-level goal, something which you could never achieve on your own as an early years provider, but which you consider to be a potential inspiration, a catalyst to get your team, parents and other relevant professionals and colleagues working together. For example, in 2010, the Departments for Education and for Health jointly stated that at the end of the EYFS, 'children should start school healthy, happy, communicative, sociable, curious, active, and ready and equipped for the next phase of life and learning' (DfE, 2011). An aim like this is something which you could cite when talking with parents, when planning a joint piece of work with health visitors, or when talking to the parks and leisure department about the need for local play areas for young children or swimming sessions for under-fives. You could refer to it at the beginning of a training day or another key time when you have your whole team together and you want to remind everyone of the bigger picture. Of course, this statement needs to be something which you develop, create and own together: the example cited is only a starting point, to give you an idea.

On the other hand, your objectives should set out what you can achieve, or make progress towards, as a team. Your objectives will be revisited more often, and may be revised in the light of changing circumstances. They can inform, at the top level, your improvement plan.

The example below shows how an early years team in a primary school with a nursery and reception class used an approach modified from Results Based Accountability to begin thinking about their objectives.

Case study: How an early years team developed and articulated their shared core purpose

Practitioners worked in pairs; the whole process took less than an hour, and they were encouraged to use Post-it notes and jot down their top three ideas after brainstorming. The rule was, that for every statement jotted down, there had to be measurement or evaluation of how well the early years team was doing: otherwise, these would just be fine words.

What do we want to make better, for children and their parents, through our work as an early years team?	Give children the best possible start.
	Happy time in nursery.
	Help children develop their early communication.
	Confidence for children.
	Healthy children who enjoy being outdoors.
	Give children a chance to develop their creativity and individual ways of learning.
	Help the most disadvantaged.
	Fully include children with special needs and disabilities.
	Involve parents in their children's learning.
	Welcome every parent.
	Children will be ready for school, good transitions, extra help to start reception where it is needed.

The manager took this short set of notes away and developed a rough statement of the setting's objectives, using bullet points:

- Help children to develop:
  - their early communication;
  - positive relationships and confidence;
  - their ability to make healthy choices.

(Continued)

(Continued)

- Encourage a real partnership with parents, sharing and discussing knowledge about the child and ways to help the child's learning and wellbeing.
- Include children with special needs and disabilities.
- Offer learning outdoors and off-site frequently and regularly.
- Help the most disadvantaged children to make accelerated progress in their learning, to narrow the gap between them and the rest.
- Promote equality and fairness.
- Support each child and family through the process of transition, so children make a confident and happy start at school.
- At the next meeting, the team worked from these notes and developed an overall vision statement:

What happens early, matters for a lifetime

We are here to help every child have a happy and healthy early childhood. We want every child to start school communicative, sociable, curious, active, and ready and equipped for the next phase of life and learning.

We offer provision which is effective for young children and their families, according to the best research: a play-based curriculum with a strong focus on early communication and positive relationships, and help for children to learn about making healthy choices.

We work in partnership with families and other professionals to support the development of our local community.

We support every child as an individual. We help every child to grow up feeling confident about their own identity, in a spirit of friendship, understanding fairness and the rights of others, valuing diversity, and ready to be a British citizen.

We are inclusive and we believe that it is good for everyone when children with disabilities and special needs go to their local early years setting.

We value parental engagement in children's learning and recognise that parents and carers are the most important people in a child's life. We can only offer the best for every child if we can work together, in a spirit of partnership.

To enrich children's learning, we are committed to learning outdoors and in the wider community, providing regular and frequent educational visits and off-site experiences.

A process like this will involve handling disagreements, making compromises, and being disciplined about making sure that a realistic set of objectives are generated which can be measured or evaluated. But, by having clear objectives and being able to track progress, teams can gain something wonderful: a sense of working together to a common purpose, and making life better for children and their families. I would argue that this is how teams gain their energy and resilience: it is far more important than any number of motivational speeches or team-bonding away days.

Coaching: Develop the professionalism of your team and identify future leaders

Coaching is a really important topic in its own right, so this section can only act as a quick introduction. If you want to know more, there are some excellent books and courses for staff working in schools and early years settings, perhaps most notably *Mentoring–Coaching: A Guide for Education Professionals* by Roger Pask and Barrie Joy (2007).

Approaches which draw on the practice and theory of coaching begin with the conviction that dialogue is generally a more powerful way of learning than simply 'being told'. Clearly, that is not always the case: when you are new in a job, or you are struggling, you may well need someone to tell you what to do, or show you and then help you to copy them. When I need to access a new computer system at work, I do not want extended dialogue with the technician, I want them to show me what to do.

But, as the researcher Julie Starr has argued, this is a limiting approach to leadership and management:

> Traditional approaches to managing people simply do not work. Being directive, i.e. 'I tell you what to do and when to do it' inhibits development of the individual over time. Staff continually instructed by overly directive managers do not blossom, they wither. When we tell staff how to do everything, we are actually teaching them to do less for themselves. (Starr, 2004)

You could adopt more of a coaching style by resisting the urge to solve problems for staff when they come to you, or the desire just to tell staff exactly how you want things done. This could apply to a brief discussion, not just to a longer 'coaching session' (which you would need proper training to offer). For example, when a member of staff asks, 'What should I do about the problem of some of the boys' behaviour outside?' you could respond with some questions to clarify the issues and to prompt more thinking:

- What are the problems you've noticed?
- Do they happen all the time or just some of the time?
- Is there anything different about the times when you don't have the problems?
- What are your thoughts about what you might do?

Discussions like this can be limited to just five to ten minutes, and they provide a space for people to think, clarify problems and try out ideas. Overall, this can help staff members to become more independent and capable: but it means giving up some of *your* power to direct activities and find solutions, in favour of creating space for people to try out their own ideas and take the lead themselves in solving a problem or developing practice.

Similarly, it is common for managers and leaders in the early years to observe staff practice and then to give a verdict:

> That was good because you made sure you looked after the care needs of your key children, and took an individual approach to changing each child's nappy when needed, and had special routines and songs for individual children.

But research into developing effective teaching has suggested that it is much more important to enable professional dialogue to take place following an observation, rather than simply issuing a judgement and then allowing a response. A judgement might reinforce a practitioner's belief that they are doing the right thing (or, on the other hand, undermine their confidence about what they are doing) but it is not an opportunity for learning. And when these observations are 'high stakes' – for example, they are linked to pay – people are likely to feel under far too much pressure to learn anything. Instead, as Robert Coe and others have argued, a much more powerful model prioritises dialogue after any observation, with a focus on outcomes for the children. This should take place in an environment of professional learning and support. It should focus mostly on the children's learning, rather than on what the practitioner did (Coe et al., 2014). Pressure and grading can create a 'performance culture' which can be effective in setting and maintaining certain standards; but I am arguing for a 'learning culture' in which individuals and teams are able to make decisions and try things out, as long as they focus on the outcomes for the children.

In summary, drawing on coaching approaches will mean that you give staff members more time to talk, and you will spend more time listening. You will be encouraging people to think out loud and to find their own possible solutions to problems, and you will be interested to follow up on how well their plans work out. In doing all of this, you will be giving team members more scope to innovate, and to lead with your support, rather than just follow your directions. As I argued above, everyone is an 'incomplete leader' – and this way, you can draw on the strengths and talents of others.

Peer observation

A formal system of peer observation is a highly effective way of sharing and developing best practice, and encouraging robust dialogue between team members about effective care and teaching. Peer observation is an approach which needs to be set up carefully, because if two practitioners are observing each other's work, the desire to be a good colleague can overwhelm the aim of providing honest and accurate feedback. A way round this is to work in threes, but this will require booking supply staff or using students to provide cover if you are a large team, or finding creative and flexible ways round if you are a small team of less than four. Peer observation in threes involves a group getting together and agreeing a focus: what aspect of care or teaching do they wish to improve, or do they need to improve following a review or an Ofsted inspection? If, for example, the focus for improvement is the use of mathematical language in the sand area, then the group would first work together on this. That might involve changes to resourcing and organisation, and brainstorming some of the language and mathematical concepts which should be developed. One or more of the three should then research the area, maybe observing effective practice in another school or setting, or reading up on the subject. This new information would be shared and, where appropriate, modelled in action. Once these cycles of activity are completed, then each member of the group of three would be observed by the other two putting those new approaches and strategies in action. With two people observing, feedback is much more likely to be accurate, because it is not coming just from one individual's perspective. Throughout, the focus is on how the group of three can work together to improve an area of practice: in this way, the approach encourages collaboration, as well as a focus on each team member's individual practice.

Table 3.7 gives an example of a peer observation form in action.

Table 3.7

Date: *April 25th, 2014*
Area of practice selected for development: *Maths in the sand tray*
Why has this area been selected? (Ofsted report, review, because children's progress/attainment is lower in this area?) *Ofsted (2013): 'Use the sand area more fully to provide even more practical opportunities for the more able children to consider mathematical concepts, such as weight, measures and capacity.'*
Team members involved *Faye, Ali and Fatima*
Practical plan: e.g. when will you discuss this? Do you need to visit another setting? Do you need reading/researching time? *Discussion time: Tuesday 10-11 a.m.* *Visit - Ali booked to visit the nursery class at Ferndown Primary (Teaching School - outstanding teaching programme) on Tuesday afternoon* *Reading/research - Fatima to read* Foundations of Mathematics: An Active Approach to Number, Shape and Measures in the Early Years *by Judith Stevens and Carole Skinner* Cover arrangements needed: *Tuesday morning: students + 1 agency* *Tuesday afternoon: agency to cover Ali*

(Continued)

Table 3.7 (Continued)

Action plan (maximum of three areas to work on improving together)
1. *Create and display a list of mathematical language to use in the area (Fatima).*   2. *Improve the resources and organisation, based on visit to Ferndown (Ali).*   3. *Practitioners to use more mathematical language and explain more mathematical concepts whilst playing with children.*

Brief peer observation notes linked to the action plan		
Faye observed using 'more', 'bigger', 'heavier'. Possible missed opportunity to extend problem-solving when child could have been challenged on how many teaspoons of sand would be needed to fill smallest pot.	*Ali observed introducing challenging language like 'estimate' and suggesting that there would be 'too many grains of sand to count'. Sometimes, opportunities for children to talk about what they were doing were interrupted by Ali using a lot of mathematical language.*	*Fatima helped children to explore and play purposefully with the new resources. Missed chances to ask children to talk about how heavy the different containers felt when full of sand.*

Evaluative note on the improvements made
Display and resources have been updated. We are starting to use mathematical language more when playing with the children, and we are using consistent terms from the list.

Next steps?
Consider the sorts of problems children might be challenged to solve, e.g. the 'guess the number of teaspoons' challenge at Ferndown (to fill different sizes of containers).

Staff who are at the early stages of their career may well need a great deal of support and guidance. They may need, like Chloe, to see effective practice modelled in some areas so they can learn step-by-step how to replicate it. This will also be true of staff who may be experienced, but are not yet fully effective. Often, we wish that staff would improve just by being around good models, or by working harder: generally, if this were the case, it would have already happened. The fact that a member of staff is not yet as good as they need to be, tells you that you need to give them more support and guidance. Instead of wasting your energy on frustration, channel it into effective performance management and training plans.

As staff become more effective, it will become necessary to give them more space for their professional development. As a manager, you cannot be there at every step to suggest how they might develop further: you need them to become more confident and self-directed. You need them to feel confident about challenging professional dialogue within their team, so that peer observation systems will improve practice and not just consist of woolly feedback to each other. In turn, as staff develop their professionalism like this, you will need them to widen their horizons and to see effective practice in other set-tings and schools. You will need to give them permission to innovate – this will mean tolerating things going wrong, as long as staff come together, review what happened and learn. If everyone just sticks to your setting's approach and is afraid to innovate, your improvement will proceed at the pace of a snail.

Conclusions

In this first part of the book, I have argued that once your provision is securely meeting the statutory requirements for the EYFS, you should focus on devel-oping the professionalism of the team as the main way to improve quality, ensure that children have an appropriate experience and secure the best possible outcomes.

Professional staff in the early years have the competence, and the space, to make decisions which are based on the best available evidence, and that suit the particular conditions in which they are working. There is no simple 'pro-gramme' for high-quality early education and care: what works in one part of the country, may not be appropriate somewhere else. For me, what is always important is that we make a positive difference to every child. Those children who are traditionally vulnerable in our education system – from poorer back-grounds, or minority groups, or with special needs – can gain lifelong benefits from experiencing high-quality early education and care. If we cannot ensure that more vulnerable children make accelerated progress in the early years, then we are putting them at risk of lagging behind the rest of the population through their schooling and beyond. Quality and equality go together.

At the top level, Ofsted exists to provide public accountability for the large sums of public money and effort that are spent on early education and care. I see the process of an Ofsted inspection as a way of testing, challenging and checking each provider's own capacity to evaluate how well they are doing, and to prioritise the improvements that are needed. There is also evidence to suggest that Ofsted have succeeded in making early years provision safer and more consistent.

The next part of this book takes a close look at Ofsted's new Common Inspection Framework (Ofsted, 2015b), which, for the first time, uses the same descriptors for all early years provision in schools and settings. As I have already argued, high-quality provision is developed by strong management and leadership which prioritises building a well-qualified and professional team. Practitioners and settings should take a confident stance towards Ofsted; we should not live in fear of inspection. The inspection framework cannot and should not be used as a guide to practice, and we should not focus on 'pleasing Ofsted': don't let the tail wag the dog.

PART 2

OFSTED'S COMMON INSPECTION FRAMEWORK FOR THE EARLY YEARS

In Part 1, I argued that developing the professionalism, knowledge, skills and confidence of your team is the best way to work towards ensuring that children have an appropriate experience of early education and care. Ofsted's inspection frameworks, evaluation schedules and your actual Ofsted inspection are all just measures. They exist to help keep children safe, and to make us accountable for the public money we use and to the parents of the children. But they do not, in themselves, help us make things any better.

Ofsted measure certain things which are important at certain times, but their current framework cannot be seen as the final word on quality. In the nursery school which I lead, we use lots of different measures to help us evaluate how well we are doing: information from Ofsted, parent consultations, indicators of children's wellbeing and thinking, the Environmental Rating Scales (ITERS-R, ECERS-3 and ECERS-E) audits, and assessment information showing how well the children progress at nursery and through their primary education.

It is for you to decide how much data and how many measures to use, balancing usefulness with manageability. You do not want to spend all your time analysing data and other measures; nor do you want to over-rely on one single source of information.

This second part of the book focusses sharply on Ofsted's new Common Inspection Framework and judgements. It is essential to be confident and knowledgeable as you approach and then experience an Ofsted inspection: it is a high-stakes event, and will result in a public judgement which has the potential to influence hugely the opinions of parents, colleagues and many others. If it goes well, you are likely to feel the satisfaction of having the hard work of you and your team publicly celebrated. But if it goes badly, and you are judged less than Good, you may not only be left with a demoralised team and a management headache; you might also have to face loss of public funding and the problems associated with reduced occupancy. You will also face more regular inspections from Ofsted if you are graded at Requires Improvement or below. Of course, being inspected sooner might well benefit you if you have taken stock of Ofsted's findings and have worked swiftly to improve your provision, gain a higher grade and make things better for the children.

4

Ofsted's new Common Inspection Framework

Ofsted introduced a radically new approach to inspection in September 2015. Instead of having different frameworks for different sectors, like early years providers and secondary schools, it now has a single Common Inspection Framework. Gill Jones, Ofsted's Deputy Director of Early Education, argues that this will bring 'more consistency to the way we judge all provision offering education for children and learners'. However, she accepts that a 'one-size-fits-all' approach would not be appropriate and states that Ofsted:

> have ensured that our early years framework reflects the age of the children in early years provision. For example, we've ensured that the framework fully reflects provision for babies and toddlers, and the new 'outcomes' judgement will focus heavily on the progress children make, given their starting points. (Ofsted, 2015a)

Gill Jones's statement reflects Ofsted's current emphasis on the *progress* of individual children and groups of children, rather than just their levels of attainment. Where children are making strong and sustained progress, then outcomes will be positively judged. You will need to have an accurate and robust system to assess children when they first start with you, drawing on information from their parents and from their previous setting (if applicable).

However, despite that reassurance, the new judgements will feel strange and probably rather uncomfortable to many professionals working in the early years. They are: outcomes; teaching, learning and assessment; personal development, behaviour and welfare; and the effectiveness of leadership and management. Drawing on these four judgements, Ofsted will grade your overall effectiveness.

Ofsted continues to have two significantly different ways of inspecting in the early years, even though both are covered by the Common Inspection Framework.

Private, voluntary and independent early years settings are generally inspected every four years under Sections 49 and 50 of the Childcare Act (2006). New settings are inspected within 30 months of their registration. Ofsted gives settings half a day's notice of inspection, and the inspection itself will generally last for a day. However, there are some exceptions to these general rules:

- **Complaint-driven inspections:** Ofsted will prioritise inspections and/or inspect more frequently when it receives a concern about a setting. Concerns trigger Ofsted to undertake a risk assessment which may conclude that an inspection is needed.

- **Three strikes and you could be out:** If a setting has been judged Inadequate it will be re-inspected within six months. After two consecutive judgements that a setting is Inadequate, if the setting is found to be Inadequate at a subsequent third inspection Ofsted may take steps to cancel registration.

- **The expectation that all early years provision should be Good, or better:** If a setting is judged to Require Improvement, it will be re-inspected within twelve months.

The government has decided to subject schools to a very different system, which varies considerably according to the type of school and the last inspection outcome:

- **Schools judged to be Good at their previous inspection** will receive a one-day short inspection under Section 8 of the Education Act (2005) approximately every three years. This short inspection will be converted into a full inspection if there are indications that the school might be Outstanding, or might Require Improvement.

- **Schools judged to be Outstanding at their previous inspection** are exempt from inspection, unless concerns arise about the performance of the school and Ofsted's risk assessment judges that an inspection is needed. However, this does not apply to maintained nursery schools or special schools, which are inspected every three years.

- **Schools judged to Require Improvement** will continue to be subject to full inspections, generally lasting for two days, under Section 5 of the Education Act (2005). Any school judged to Require Improvement will also be subject to monitoring inspection visits, led by one of Her Majesty's Inspectorate. A monitoring visit is reported on through a letter to the headteacher, which is published on Ofsted's website.

- **Schools judged to be Inadequate** also remain subject to full inspections and a more intensive cycle of monitoring inspections led by Her Majesty's Inspectorate.

These differences have been outlined in brief here: full details of all the different arrangements are explained on Ofsted's website.

Any school or setting can be inspected at no notice if there is a serious and urgent concern, for example about safeguarding.

The pages that follow explore Ofsted's new framework, considering how it applies to early years education and care. As well as helping you to prepare for your inspection over time, I will also suggest some strategies to help you to manage the actual inspection event, from the moment you get the phone call to the final meeting at the end, and offer some advice about what you might do if things start to go wrong.

A new approach to inspection

Perhaps the first thing you need to know about the new Common Inspection Framework is that Ofsted are very explicit now about not advocating any particular approaches to care, teaching and learning. In fact, as long ago as 2013, Sir Michael Wilshaw, formerly Her Majesty's Chief Inspector of Schools, said that: 'it is not for Ofsted to say "that is the right way of teaching and that is the wrong way of teaching"' (Stewart, 2013). That message is now made absolutely clear in many of Ofsted's publications, including the *School Inspection Handbook* (2015d) and *Early Years Inspection Handbook* (2015e), which both state that: 'inspectors must not advocate a particular method of planning, teaching or assessment'. It is not so long ago that many conversations between managers and practitioners and messages from training sessions and conferences would begin with a phrase like, 'Ofsted want to see ....' There were all sorts of rumours about what sort of practice inspectors would, and would not like. That has all changed now. Instead, Ofsted are really only interested in one thing: is what you are doing effective, or not? Whatever your approach to organisation, care and teaching, Ofsted will only be interested in whether they can find the evidence that it works.

Another important change follows through from that: Ofsted will no longer grade your teaching. So, you can safely forget all about those books, courses, theories and rumours about what you need to do in order to be judged an Outstanding teacher. Instead of grading your teaching, Ofsted will only be interested in the overall impact of teaching over time. Are children making good progress in their learning and developing their skills? Are you having a positive impact on their personal development and behaviour, and their Spiritual, Moral, Social and Cultural Development?

It can be argued that this change in Ofsted's approach is a good thing for leaders and managers in the early years. It makes it very clear that our roles are now very different to the roles of Ofsted inspectors. Our job is to develop the overall culture, and to provide support, encouragement and guidance to staff individually. It definitely is our role to make judgements about how well individual staff members are caring for the children and teaching them, and how well the team work together to create provision which is appropriate, and which is improving. Equally, I would argue that the days of leaders and managers conducting mock inspections and applying Ofsted-style gradings should be allowed to become a blur in the past. Strong leaders will work hard with their teams to improve the provision for the sake of the children; weaker leaders will invoke Ofsted's authority instead of their own, causing staff to feel alarmed and stressed by the prospect of an inspection and pushing for changes 'because that's what Ofsted want'.

However, it is worth noting that schools have less scope to choose their own approach to teaching and learning in the early years because the EYFS is statutory. It sets out, in law, certain approaches to early years education and care which are legal requirements. So, Ofsted does not advocate formal teaching or play-based learning. But the Statutory Framework quite clearly states that: 'play is essential for children's development … Children learn by leading their own play, and by taking part in play which is guided by adults.' So, if you are not providing play-based learning in the EYFS, then you could ultimately be found to be breaking the law. That applies to lots of other aspects of the EYFS. For example, you cannot simply make your own decisions about how to organise staff to support children's Personal, Social and Emotional Development: you must have a key person system. Unless you have gained an exemption from the Department for Education (DfE), you must by law follow every aspect of the EYFS Statutory Framework. As one of Ofsted's most important roles is to uphold the law and to check compliance with statutory requirements, you are likely to find that there is a significant focus on the framework. If you are in a school, you may need to explain this to colleagues who are not early years specialists.

An overview of the Common Inspection Framework

Ofsted state that their inspection, regulation and indeed all their work is intended to encourage services 'to improve, to be user-focused and to be efficient and effective in their use of resources' (Ofsted, 2015b). On the one hand, the new framework argues strongly for the objectivity of the new inspection process, which uses a range of evidence evaluated against a framework and then provides a 'diagnosis of what should improve'. Whether it is really possible to achieve this level of accuracy, given all the human and social factors at play, is a question which is left unconsidered.

Importantly, the framework cautions inspectors against merely complying with the relevant approaches to gathering evidence and making judgements, saying that they must seek to be 'curious as well as compliant'. That focus on 'curious' implies, first of all, that inspectors may, where they judge it necessary, follow lines of inquiry in a way in which you might not have predicted. You might be very well prepared for a focus on children's progress and outcomes. But, if an inspector sees young children becoming distressed and no sign of support or comfort from their key person, and no feedback to parents about the child's experiences, then their focus might quickly shift to checking whether children are adequately cared for and safeguarded, and whether you are implementing an adequate key person approach. The emphasis on the inspector's curiosity also implies that the process of inspection must be informed by professional judgement and experience – it can't just be done 'by the book'. That focus on professionalism implies something further: that leaders and everyone else on the staff team should engage in professional dialogue with inspectors, explaining (where it is practicable) what they are doing, why they are doing it that way, and what they know about the impact. Curious inspectors will work best with staff who are themselves curious and confident to engage in professional dialogue and consider questions and uncertainties. This is discussed further in Chapter 6.

I would argue that this emphasis on professional dialogue is preferable to the type of over-preparation which results in inspectors being bombarded with written information, evidence and data in order to close down dialogue and discussion. That approach is stressful both to staff and to the inspector – and Ofsted now explicitly ask providers to 'minimise disruption, stress and bureaucracy'.

Although there is a Common Inspection Framework, there will still be two quite different groups of inspectors in the early years. School provision will be the remit of inspectors directly recruited and employed by Ofsted. This group of inspectors will most likely have the highest levels of qualifications and training, but are likely to have the least direct experience in the early years. Very few will have any experience of working with three- and four-year-olds, let alone two-year-olds. So, whilst there is a Common Inspection Framework, their perspective will be shaped by their experience which will generally be school-based, with more expertise in respect to older children. Early years provision will initially be the remit of inspectors from private companies like Tribal and Prospects, who have contracts with Ofsted to carry out inspections. They are likely to be less qualified than Ofsted's directly employed inspectorate, but more likely to have experience of working with young children (including those aged up to three years old) in private, voluntary and community settings. Although this group of inspectors will be moved into the direct employment of Ofsted from April 2017, the differences in professional background and experience will remain the same.

Quick guide: What has changed under the Common Inspection Framework?

For schools

The key differences for schools are:

- The addition of a separate early years judgement.

- The inclusion of provision for two-year-olds in the school framework: you will no longer have a separate childcare inspection if you directly manage provision for two-year-olds.

The other changes to the Ofsted *School Inspection Handbook* (2015d) have generally developed out of the previous framework, rather than marking a wholly new approach.

The quickest way to see what is 'common' in the new Common Inspection Framework for the early years, is by comparing the grade descriptors in the Early Years section of the *School Inspection Handbook* to the grade descriptors in the *Early Years Inspection Handbook*. They reflect each other. This means that, for the first time, it makes sense to have a single book like this one to consider Ofsted's approach to inspecting the early years across all sectors. It also means that it is useful for school EYFS leaders to read the *Early Years Inspection Handbook*, because in places it gives more details which can help to explain the grade descriptors.

One of the implications of the separate early years judgement in school inspections, is that the leadership of the EYFS will be considered when Ofsted make their judgement about the school's leadership. Where EYFS co-ordinators are considered to be 'middle leaders' in the school, there will be an expectation that a senior leader is closely involved in early years. A Requires Improvement judgement for the early years would very likely be reflected in the judgement for leadership and management overall, and probably in the judgement about the school's overall effectiveness. The EYFS has become a higher priority.

Many schools will no longer have a full inspection, just a one-day Section 8 inspection. However, for Ofsted to validate the school's own judgement of its effectiveness, the EYFS will need to have a high priority. Inspectors may not spend much time in the early years, but they will expect to see accurate and sufficiently detailed self-evaluation of the quality and effectiveness of the school's EYFS provision. If the short inspection highlights possible flaws in your self-evaluation, it will be converted into a full inspection which could result in downgrading. Her Majesty's Chief Inspector of Schools, Sir Michael Willshaw, cautioned in March 2016 that: 'in the minority of schools that went down a grade or more, inspectors ... often found an overly generous self-assessment of the school by governors and senior leaders that was not supported by evidence'. You will want to be sure that your self-evaluation and action planning to improve are effective, so that your school will not fall into this small, but hardly select, group.

Maintained nursery schools will be judged against the first five areas in the *School Inspection Handbook*, not just the early years section.

Because of the consistency across the Common Inspection Framework, this book takes the *School* and the *Early Years Inspection Handbooks* as its starting points. This offers EYFS leads and co-ordinators a detailed discussion of what Ofsted are looking for.

For private, voluntary and independent early years settings

Whilst the Common Inspection Framework represents an evolution in Ofsted's approach for schools, it is closer to a revolution for settings. The key differences are:

- **Notification of inspection:** Instead of the no-notice regime, settings will generally have a half-day's notice.

- **Extremism and radicalisation:** Inspectors will check how you are safeguarding children from violent extremism, in line with the Prevent agenda.

- **Fundamental British values:** Settings will be expected to show how they promote British values, including tolerance and respect, rule of law, individual liberty and democracy, in a way which is suitable to the age and development of the children.

- **Early Years Pupil Premium:** Settings will be expected to show how they are spending this in order to narrow the gap between disadvantaged children and the rest, and how they are evaluating the impact of their activities.

- **Monitoring attendance:** Inspectors will check the attendance of children on roll and what steps you take to improve the attendance of those who are frequently absent – because absence could be a safeguarding concern.

- **Measuring the progress of different groups of children:** You will be expected to show that you know about the progress of specific groups (for example, boys and girls; children speaking English as an additional language; children with special educational needs and disabilities). Where there are differences in progress, Ofsted will check what actions you are taking to narrow those gaps, and how effective your actions have been.

All of these significant changes are discussed in more detail below.

Reflection point

In Part 1, you were encouraged to reflect on what phase of development your setting was at:

- **Phase one:** Practice which works for you.

- **Phase two:** Practice which works for you, and is consistent with the research and evidence base.

- **Phase three:** Developing leading-edge practice.

Whatever your phase of development, it is essential that you quickly meet the expectations outlined above. For example, if you are an early years setting, then you need to adapt to new Ofsted requirements like monitoring and following up poor attendance, tracking progress and promoting British values immediately. If you do not, you risk a judgement which is less than Good – with all the reputational and funding damage that could cause. Likewise, if you are a school, you need to understand and respond to the implications of the separate EYFS judgement. Even if you are in a Good or Outstanding school, you need to have accurate self-evaluation information which is specific to your early years provision.

5

The Common Inspection Framework

Effectiveness of leadership and management

Introduction

Ofsted's new approach to evaluating leadership and management largely builds on their previous inspection frameworks, but there are some important and challenging new elements to contend with.

We often think of leadership in terms of drive, inspiration and charisma. Successful leadership also requires strong management techniques, like having systems and policies in place. But it is important to note that Ofsted's key concern when inspecting leadership and management is 'effectiveness' – not personality, not drive, not the number of hours you have worked, and not the weight of your management documents. Typically, your Ofsted inspector will not just check that you have an appropriate safeguarding policy, but will want to know what difference it is making to the children in your setting. How do you ensure that staff follow sound procedures, and how do you know whether those procedures are helping to keep children safe?

The framework has a sharp focus on the curriculum and how the learning opportunities and the culture of the provision are improving the life chances of children, especially the most disadvantaged. Ofsted are also looking for your ambition: do you have really high expectations of what your team can achieve, and how you can change things for the better, for the children and families you work with?

In the sections below, I will consider how you can align your evidence and self-evaluation with the EYFS Statutory Framework, which is the legal basis for the new Ofsted framework.

There are three other statutory areas which will influence how Ofsted grade your leadership and management. Safeguarding has always been a major concern for Ofsted, and in the recent period there has been much rapid change in the legislation. You absolutely have to keep up with the changing laws and expectations, both to ensure that you are doing everything you can to keep children safe and well, and also to ensure that your approach is judged to be effective by Ofsted. Safeguarding is not graded: you are expected to get it right.

There has also been a significant change in how Ofsted relate to leaders and managers in the early years: there is a much higher level of engagement now. For early years provision in the private, voluntary and independent sector, the 'Ofsted Big Conversation' has brought together Ofsted's regional leads with local managers and owners to have dialogue about the inspection framework and controversial topics like complaint-driven inspections. Ofsted also post research, guidance and videos online about early years practice across the sectors.

Finally, it cannot be stressed too much that there is more to being an effective leader and manager than simply trying to succeed against Ofsted's framework. Much of leadership is about motivation, encouragement, coaching, being resilient when things go wrong, and always being open to learning from mistakes. Ofsted can validate (or challenge) your own evaluation, but they do not and cannot provide a step-by-step recipe book for improvement. So, it is important to focus on your own professional learning and development in this area. Ofsted exists to hold us accountable to parents and to the wider public – we are responsible for our own professionalism and for creating a culture of continuous learning.

Evaluating and demonstrating the impact of your leadership and management

Compliance

The starting point here is compliance. The Statutory Framework sets out the policies which you are required to have. If you are a school, you do not need separate EYFS policies, as long as the requirements are already met through an existing policy. But if you are an early years setting, then you will need to have all of the policies and they must be easy to access. You also need to be certain that you are complying with all the legislation relating to safeguarding, employment, anti-discrimination, health and safety, and data collection.

Your inspector will not check all of these policies. However, if matters of concern come up during the inspection, or if any of these policies are not adequate, then your inspector may well look in more detail. That can create a high level of stress during an inspection, so you would be well advised to make sure that everything is right and proper before you face all that pressure and scrutiny.

The inspector *will* check every Disclosure and Barring Service (DBS) record and every paediatric first aid certificate.

The inspection will undoubtedly look very closely at your safeguarding policies and practice to check that they are effective. Safeguarding is not graded by Ofsted – you must meet the minimum standards or else you will be judged Inadequate. Generally, if a small problem comes to light – with your policies, for example, or your Single Central Record – Ofsted will make a proportionate judgement. If it does not materially affect the safety of the children on roll, then it is unlikely to cause a problem. So, if all the checks are being carried out properly on staff before they are employed, but one person's checks are filed away but missed off the record, you are likely to be given advice to improve your Single Central Record. That advice might be noted in your report. But you would not be found Inadequate, because children have been safeguarded by your checking process. However, if a member of staff were missing from your Single Central Record, and you had no evidence that you had checked their suitability, then your safeguarding would be Inadequate.

Safeguarding

Just as you must show your compliance with statutory regulations, you must also demonstrate that you are effective at safeguarding children. If you are leading the early years in a school, then safeguarding will be judged across the whole school. But the EYFS will play a particularly important part in this, because the youngest children are the most vulnerable.

At the time of writing, Ofsted summarised their guidance in the publication *Inspecting Safeguarding in Early Years, Education and Skills Settings* which is available online (Ofsted, 2015c). However, whilst the overall approach outlined in this document is unlikely to change, there may be updates since the time of publication so you would be advised to check online for the most recent guidance.

It might be helpful to think about safeguarding under five major headings:

- Having appropriate policies and procedures for safeguarding.
- Keeping children safe and well in your setting.
- Ensuring that staff are regularly trained.
- Staff recruitment and vetting.
- Working in partnership with others to keep children safe and well.

Overall, you need to consider not just your compliance, but also the *impact* of those five areas of work.

Appropriate policies and procedures

You may wish to check with your local Safeguarding Board to see if they have a model safeguarding policy which you can use and adapt:

- If you are a school, the policy must comply with the requirements of the Department for Education document *Keeping Children Safe in Education*. Check that you are using the most up to date version of this policy, and ensure that all staff have read Section One and that they have signed a document to confirm that they have read it (www.gov.uk/government/publications/keeping-children-safe-in-education-2).

- All early years providers, regardless of the sector, must comply with the government's *Working Together to Safeguard Children* document (www.gov.uk/government/publications/working-together-to-safeguard-children-2) and with the *Prevent Duty Guidance* for England and Wales (www.gov.uk/government/publications/prevent-duty-guidance).

- Everyone must also comply with the safeguarding duties set out in the *Statutory Framework for the Early Years Foundation Stage* (2014 version) (www.gov.uk/government/uploads/system/uploads/attachment_data/file/335504/EYFS_frame-work_from_1_September_2014__with_clarification_note.pdf) and the *Disqualification under the Childcare Act 2006* statutory guidance (www.gov.uk/government/publications/disqualification-under-the-childcare-act-2006).

Simply having these policies is not enough. You need to make sure that all staff members are familiar with the key points and have access to all these documents. You could have a special shelf for safeguarding documents, or put everything into the same folder on a shared drive if your system is IT-based. It is also important that you make all parents and other users aware of your policies. For example, you might have a short section about safeguarding in your information pack for parents or on your website, and make it easy for parents to access the full policy. Having a dusty folder on a high shelf won't do.

In summary, you need to have the policies which comply with the regulations, they need to be easy to access, and everyone needs regular reminders about them. Anyone who has a concern should know how to raise it, and will expect a prompt and effective response from the safeguarding team or co-ordinator. If a referral is made to Children's Social Care, the safeguarding co-ordinator will expect a timely and appropriate response, and will persist in following up concerns as often as necessary.

Keeping children safe and well in your setting

Working Together to Safeguard Children defines safeguarding and promoting the welfare of children as:

- Protecting children from maltreatment.

- Preventing impairment of children's health or development.

- Ensuring that children are growing up in circumstances consistent with the provision of safe and effective care.

- Taking action to enable all children to have the best outcomes.

That can make it sound as if safeguarding is mostly about noticing signs or symptoms of possible child abuse. Whilst that certainly is an important aspect of safeguarding, you also need to think very carefully about the minute-by-minute running of your own setting. In this respect, safeguarding includes how well you care for children in the broadest sense. Does your key person approach plan for close and responsive relationships between children and their key people, helping each child feel emotionally secure and confident that there is someone special who will help them, comfort them, and (depending on their age) listen to what they say or show using their body language? Your approach to intimate care routines, like nappy-changing, needs to be clearly set out in a policy document and agreed by all staff. The procedures you adopt need to be appropriate, so that children are kept safe. You will need to think about the messages that children will be receiving if nappy-changing or toileting is carried out by large numbers of people, and not largely undertaken by their key person – will they get the message that their body and privacy are respected, or the message that almost anyone can come along and undress them? Your health and safety and risk assessment processes need to be effective in keeping children safe in your setting (without attempting to abolish risk and challenge entirely), and you will need to consider safety from a child's-eye point of view, not just as a tick-box exercise.

A safe setting is one where children's need for emotional warmth and responsive care is promoted, and where behaviour is well managed. When managing difficult behaviour, you need to think about the possible impact on the other children, not just how you are trying to set limits – if children are being hit, bitten and scratched, are you taking every reasonable step to keep them safe in the future as well as working intensively with the child who needs to learn about acceptable ways to behave? Your approach to behaviour and to promoting children's wellbeing will explain how staff help children to learn positive ways of interacting with their peers, depending on their age and development, as well as explaining how you set limits and how you manage the rare occasions when you have to intervene physically to restrain a child.

You need robust arrangements for issues like managing medical needs, dispensing medicines and keeping children with allergies safe – both in your setting and when you go out. You need to have a clear policy around the use of mobile phones and cameras in your setting, and make sure that the policy is scrupulously enforced.

Ofsted helpfully list some of these wider issues, several of which are more pertinent to older children but all of which are relevant to the early years to some degree:

Safeguarding is not just about protecting children, learners and vulnerable adults from deliberate harm, neglect and failure to act. It relates to broader aspects of care and education, including:

- children's and learners' health and safety and well-being
- the use of reasonable force
- meeting the needs of children and learners with medical conditions

- providing first aid

- educational visits

- intimate care and emotional well-being

- online safety and associated issues

- appropriate arrangements to ensure children's and learners' security, taking into account the local context.

(Ofsted, 2015c)

It is worth considering that safeguarding concerns in these areas will often not be brought to you as a leader and manager in those terms. It is much more likely that a member of staff will share a concern about a colleague seeming to be a bit rough in her handling of the babies, or not following your key person approach or your behaviour policy. Often, your job is to listen actively and engage in dialogue with the member of staff to determine whether what you are being told is potentially damaging to the safety and wellbeing of the children on roll. If it is, then you must as a first priority think about how you will address the issue in terms of the children's experience, and not just as a tricky personnel problem or the management of variable practice. Poor practice can quickly become a safeguarding issue. For example, if children are not well managed, if staffing falls below minimum legal requirements or is not adequate to meet the children's needs, if spaces are not kept ordered and tidy, then children are at risk – even if the staff are well-meaning.

Above all else, you must do everything you can to keep children safe and well.

Where staff are concerned about the impact of poor parenting on a child, or where they are concerned that a child is presenting with signs or symptoms of abuse, there needs to be a clear reporting process. It is advisable to have a systematic approach to logging all concerns in writing, recording the judgement of the safeguarding lead, and recording the actions taken to help keep the child safe and well. Staff need to feel confident that their concerns will be listened to and acted on, and they need to know who they should talk to if they feel this is not the case. Again, not all concerns will be raised in this way, so your supervision system is an essential part of your safeguarding work. Staff need regular opportunities for supervision meetings, with a clear focus on children's welfare and wellbeing. This can allow staff to explore niggles and queries which may help their work in caring for the child in the setting, or may clarify that there is a safeguarding concern that needs acting on. If supervision time is focussed on performance and targets, then staff will not have that safe space to explore their thoughts and concerns.

Staff may often be fearful of raising concerns, in case there is a negative reaction from parents. So it is important that you reassure staff that you will support them in such cases, and that you will be on-hand should a parent be unhappy, upset or angry. Negative repercussions will quickly discourage staff from raising their concerns – so, you will need to minimise their occurrence and their impact.

Ofsted have helpfully listed the major categories of safeguarding concern in their guidance (Ofsted, 2015c). At first glance, many elements may not seem to be immediately relevant to the early years, but sometimes you need to think more widely about the safeguarding issues you may come across. Online safety might seem to apply only to older children on Facebook, but have you considered how many young children might be using their parents' mobiles or tablets, and might come across disturbing or unsuitable content on sites like YouTube? You might well find yourself working with teenage parents for whom there might be concerns around sexual exploitation, or forced marriage. In an area with gang activity, even very young children might be exposed to gang culture and you might observe that in their pretend play.

Finally, having a suitable complaints procedure for parents and other users can play an important part in making sure that your setting is safe for children. As well as making sure your policy is readily available, it is important to encourage an 'open culture' which makes parents confident to state any concerns they might have, either formally or informally. Parents may be afraid that if they complain, staff will treat them or their children differently, so you will need to provide explicit reassurance on this point. Make sure that parents know they can complain directly to the senior leader in charge of the setting, and also ensure that they know how to complain directly to Ofsted if necessary, both by displaying the Ofsted Parents Poster prominently, and by including Ofsted's contact details in your policy.

Complaints are an important part of safeguarding, because it is possible that a parent might notice something concerning which you have missed. A parent may arrive and find the main door open, or a child playing unsupervised. They may report back that their child is anxious about a member of staff, or has said something worrying. Following through on complaints makes your setting safer, either because you can reassure the parent that you have carefully looked into their concern and there is nothing to worry about, or because you have been given an early warning that something is going wrong.

Ensuring that staff are regularly trained

It is important that *all* staff are trained in safeguarding – including caretakers, premises managers, administration assistants and everyone else in contact with children and parents. You never know who will notice something of concern, and often parents have good relationships with people they see around the building, like receptionists and cleaners, and may talk to them and share important information. I certainly remember the time when a parent told a receptionist how she was at the end of her tether with her two-year-old – if the receptionist had not passed on her concerns about how stressed the parent seemed, we would never have known how much she needed help and support.

It is a requirement in schools that the safeguarding lead has child protection training every two years, and this would be advisable for all settings. Ofsted state that there should be:

> clear and effective arrangements for staff development and training in respect of the protection and care of children and learners. Staff and other adults receive regular supervision and support if they are working directly and regularly with children and learners whose safety and welfare are at risk. (Ofsted, 2015c)

Although there is no timescale here, you would be advised to schedule regular training (e.g. annual) and to ensure that all staff have safeguarding training as soon as they start, as part of their induction.

The final, important point to make is that you should draw on your recent training and the latest publications from the Department for Education and from Ofsted to guide your safeguarding approach, policies and procedures.

Staff recruitment and vetting

It is important that anyone recruiting staff to work at your setting is trained in Safe Recruitment, and follows the Safer Recruitment guidance set out in *Keeping Children Safe in Education*. Your local authority or Safeguarding Board may offer this training, or you can complete courses online (for example, search online for 'NSPCC Safer Recruitment in Education').

Your Ofsted inspection will include a detailed check to ensure that your Single Central Record is up to date and fully compliant. You will need to show that staff working with the children are 'suitable', as defined in the DfE's *Statutory Framework for the Early Years Foundation Stage* (2014: Sections 3.09 to 3.13). You need to demonstrate that you know your legal obligations in respect to Childcare Disqualification and have effective procedures to find out whether a member of staff has been disqualified. You need to be mindful that to employ a disqualified person knowingly is an offence and would lead Ofsted to judge that your safeguarding was not effective. If you have volunteers who are not DBS-checked, you will need to explain how your procedures keep the children safe, and you will need to show that you have checked with colleges and teacher training providers that all trainees have been checked and that the provider is completely open about any information it holds on its students.

'Vetting' should be understood as a continuous process. A practitioner's DBS record may be clear, and their references good, but they might still pose a risk to children that has never been detected. People can also change over time, and someone who posed no risk at the time of their recruitment might change into someone who is no longer safe to care for children.

So, as a manager and leader, you should remain alert to changes in the behaviour, conduct or circumstances of the practitioners in your team, and not be afraid or embarrassed to ask questions or to confront people when you feel uneasy or concerned. If you are worried about someone's emotional wellbeing or mental health, you need to talk about your worries and consider how you might offer support – just like you would if someone was returning to work with a broken arm. Equally, staff should know how to raise concerns about the conduct of a colleague, and how to share information they may come by about a colleague's conduct out of work which may raise a question about their suitability to work with children. This touches on whistleblowing and ensuring that staff know of their obligation to raise and pursue concerns irrespective of friendships, team loyalty, or not wishing to question the judgement or conduct of someone who is senior to them. Safeguarding must always override every other issue in the team, and it is useful to remind everyone regularly of this.

Working in partnership to keep children safe and well

Checking on your partnership arrangements has two basic strands. Firstly, your policies and procedures should make it clear how you work with external agencies if you have a concern. For example, if you were concerned that a child was being neglected, how did you pass that concern to your local Children's Social Care team? You need to make sure you are using the referral system promoted by your local Safeguarding Board, that you include all relevant details in your referral, and that you follow it up. Make sure that you know what decision has been made by Children's Social Care team and what you are expected to do to help keep the child safe.

Secondly, you may be working with children with Child in Need Plans, or who are subject to Inter-Agency Child Protection. In both cases, Ofsted will check that you understand the concerns about the child's welfare or safety, know exactly what you are doing as part of the plan, and know what to do if you have further concerns.

It is also important to know about and understand your local context. You can find out about the key safeguarding issues in your area from your local Safeguarding Board. Consider what you are doing to help the Board's work in those key areas. For example, if there is a serious problem with domestic violence in your area, can you display posters and other information so that people affected know how they can get help? Have staff had specialist training in this area? You should also know about Ofsted's key judgements when they inspected your local authority's safeguarding – especially if it was found to be Inadequate, or to Require Improvement. At Sheringham Nursery School, we paid particular attention to Ofsted's finding that social workers were overwhelmed with new referrals in our local authority. So, staff had training about how to spot the signs that a family might need Early Help, and about how to offer advice or refer them on as appropriate. Where more Early Help is offered, problems can often be 'nipped in the bud' before they become too large, and this reduces the rate of referrals.

Considering the impact of your work around safeguarding

It may seem obvious to state this, but you can have excellent policies and trained staff, but your safeguarding may still not be good enough. There are numerous reviews of children's deaths or serious injuries that found no fault with training or procedures – the problem was simply that people didn't act on their knowledge, or share their concerns. There wasn't the right *culture* to keep children safe.

So, it is firstly worth reminding ourselves of how important safeguarding, in the widest sense, is for young children and how it weaves through everything else we do to help children have the best start to life. As the DfE's *Statutory Framework for the Early Years Foundation Stage* states:

> children develop quickly in the early years and a child's experiences between birth and age five have a major impact on their future life chances. A secure, safe and happy childhood is important in its own right. Good parenting and

high-quality early learning together provide the foundation children need to make the most of their abilities and talents as they grow up.

Where safeguarding is effective, leaders and managers will be checking that referrals are made speedily when necessary, but they will also go further and proactively check that all staff know what to look for, and how to act when they are concerned. Through supervision and other activities, staff will be encouraged to share and discuss any concerns they might have. Parents will be updated regularly about safeguarding and will know how they can ask for friendly support and advice, as well as knowing how to raise a concern if they have one. Your key person system, and wider approach to support children's emotional wellbeing, will ensure that children have strong relationships, know who to go to if they are upset, and will ensure that someone knows a child well enough to pick up on signs or notice changes if all is not well. Your approach to behaviour will lead to children showing positive signs of feeling safe and secure, and flourishing in their social and emotional development.

You need to have a culture of safeguarding that permeates everything you do with children, with families, and with your wider community. You also need to promote your practice: make sure that the parents and the wider community know that safeguarding is at the heart of your practice.

This systematic approach is sometimes referred to as the 'golden thread of safeguarding' (Figure 5.1) and it is worth reviewing the strengths and weaknesses in your 'thread' at least once every few months.

Figure 5.1 The 'golden thread of safeguarding'

- **Policy:** Check that your policy is compliant with current legislation and guidance. Your local Safeguarding Board may be able to help you with this. All staff should be aware of your policy, and, if it is based on a model policy, make sure that it has been adapted for your setting and not simply 'lifted'.

- **Procedures:** Check that everyone on the team is aware of the procedures and protocols set out in your policy and that these are always followed if staff are concerned about a child. It is almost inevitable that there will be times when staff have a concern but they hold it to themselves or within their team, rather than passing it on to the safeguarding lead. So, you will need to remind staff regularly about sharing concerns in meetings and through supervision.

- **Practice:** Check that practice is always effective. Are checks effective in making sure that the environment is safe and secure? Does practice ensure that children feel emotionally safe, valued and respected? Do you systematically and regularly check the welfare and safety of all children who are categorised as Children in Need or who are subject to Inter-Agency Child Protection?

- **Partners:** Check the quality and impact of your work with key partners. If a child has an allocated social worker, are you clear about your role in the social worker's current plan? Are you helping the social worker to assess whether things are improving for the child? Is your knowledge about the child's development, health and wellbeing reflected in the social worker's assessment and planning? Do you have strong relationships and regular contact with key partners, like health visitors, Children's Centre staff and social workers?

- **Impact:** Check that your work is making a difference. If staff are not raising any concerns about children for discussion, then it is almost certain that your approach is not having the impact of making staff aware and encouraging reflective and safe practice. Check whether the early help and advice you offer parents is helping them to improve their parenting. If a child is subject to Inter-Agency Child Protection, is the work you are doing with the family and the other partners leading to improved care and ensuring the child is kept safe and well? Or, if things are not improving, do you make sure the social worker is aware of your ongoing concerns? Have you asked for feedback from a social worker or social work manager about your joint work?

Reflection point

This is another moment when it may be useful to pause and consider whether you are meeting in full all of the safeguarding requirements outlined above. Whatever stage of development you are at, you are expected to keep children safe. You will be expected to comply with government requirements and advice. If you fall down in this area, you risk being found Inadequate – even if the issue seems to you to be quite technical or minor. If you have any doubts about your compliance, ask for help. Your local Safeguarding Board or Children's Social Care team may be able to recommend a consultant to help you review your approach. Advice and support is also available from professional organisations.

Secondly, always remember that effective safeguarding is not just about ticking all the boxes. It is about having an 'open culture' so that staff feel able at any time to raise their concerns, even if they may feel trivial or minor. Staff need to have the confidence and professionalism to notice and to challenge anything they feel is not in the best interests of children, without fear or favour - no matter whether a concern relates to a best friend at work, or an older and more experienced practitioner.

You may also find the following list, from a recent Serious Case Review (Plymouth Safeguarding Children Board, 2010) helpful when you are reflecting on how safe your provision is:

- Staff are respectful to all employees as well as children.

- Staff are open about discussing good and poor practice.

- Blame only happens in extreme circumstances.

- Leaders model the appropriate behaviour.

- Staff are knowledgeable about the vulnerability of the children whom they look after and aware that abusers may already be in the employ of the organisation.

- Children are listened to.

- Staff are empowered to challenge poor practice.

- Parents are encouraged to be involved in their child's plan and welcomed to the setting.

- Whistle-blowing procedures are in place and staff know how to use them.

Equality

The Equality Act (2010) legally requires early years settings to promote all forms of equality, and to help foster understanding and respect between individuals, groups and diverse communities. Ofsted take their role of checking compliance with the Act very seriously.

As well as expecting to see that you promote gender and racial equality in the early years, Ofsted will specifically look at outcomes for children including those who:

- Are disabled, have medical conditions or have special educational needs.

- Are learning English as an additional language.

- Are from gypsy, Roma and traveller backgrounds.

- Are 'looked after' (in care).

- Are 'disadvantaged', specifically those eligible for the Early Years Pupil Premium.

The full list of the outcomes which Ofsted will pay particular attention to can be found in the Common Inspection Framework. If the outcomes for some groups of children, such as those listed above, are not as good as the outcomes for the rest and you are not taking any action to address this, then you are not advancing equality of opportunity. That means that you are potentially in breach of the Equality Act (2010).

As always, Ofsted will want to focus on the effectiveness of your approach, not just the work you have done. Can you show that different groups of children all benefit from your provision and make good progress? Do you consider the experiences of groups with 'protected characteristics' (as defined in the Equality Act 2010) and ensure that children from those groups are making strong and sustained progress in your setting, or ensure that you are taking action where that is not yet the case? If you have focussed on positive images of girls and women engaging in technical and scientific activities, have you seen an impact in terms of how girls play and learn in your setting?

I would argue that promoting equality is a vital aspect of our work in the early years. Even very young children will have already picked up on the attitudes of their family and community towards people who are seen as 'different'. The advertising and selling of toys in England is also very gender-based, with separate areas in shops for boys and girls, and very different types of advertisements too. So, children may well come into early years settings with a range of views about what boys can and can't do, for example. They may be fearful of, or hostile to, children from other ethnic backgrounds or other family set-ups, like having lesbian or gay parents. But our work in the early years gives us a great opportunity to explore and confront parents' and children's attitudes. Young children do not have 'hardened' views yet: they can learn to be positive about diversity, and to reject discrimination. Two important books which explore this area further are Siraj-Blatchford (1994) and Lane (2008).

Promoting British values

Ofsted's announcement that it will inspect how well early years settings promote British values has generated a good deal of concern. It is certainly very difficult to imagine how an early years setting would explain that a set of 'values' – already a difficult concept for a young child – belongs to one country rather than another. The Foundation Years website helpfully checked this with the Department for Education and explained that 'the fundamental British values of democracy, rule of law, individual liberty, mutual respect and tolerance for those with different faiths and beliefs are already implicitly embedded in the 2014 Early Years Foundation Stage' (see www.foundationyears.org.uk/files/2015/03/Fundamental_British_Values.pdf). In particular, the Specific Area in the EYFS of 'Understanding the World' already suggests an approach to supporting children's learning in this area. Much of the traditional emphasis in the early years on helping children to learn to share, take turns, and develop an awareness of other people's feelings, can be interpreted as 'promoting British values'.

There have, perhaps, been occasions when early years practitioners have wished to respect other cultures in ways which are not helpful. For example, sometimes adults can feel that it is not polite to question people about their beliefs and cultures, whereas a more considered approach might be to encourage questioning and dialogue. I can remember an occasion when I was working in a nursery class and one child asked another child's mother about her hijab, and there was an embarrassed silence for a moment or two amongst the staff until the mother answered the questions confidently. The guidelines on the Foundation Years website clearly state that 'children should be given opportunities to develop enquiring minds in an atmosphere where questions are valued'. In settings where children come from a range of cultures, it will be important to promote values of fairness, equality and tolerance. When I was working as the Early Years Adviser in Tower Hamlets, a nursery teacher worked very sensitively with a small group of boys after she heard one of them say 'girls don't drive cars', explaining that there are many women drivers in London, and pointing out women bus drivers on a local walk. Her sensitivity went along with her firmness of purpose: she made it clear to the boys that it was not acceptable to tell girls they couldn't 'drive' the pretend bus, or crowd them out.

Remember that Ofsted will specifically report on how well you are actively promoting British values. The following checklist, based on the Foundation Years guidance (www.foundationyears.org.uk/files/2015/03/Fundamental_British_Values.pdf), can be used to help you to evaluate your work in this area:

- **Introducing the concept of democracy:** Do you give children opportunities to make decisions together?

- **Introducing the concept of the rule of law:** Do you help children to understand the rules of your setting? Depending on their age/development, can they be involved in drawing them up? Do you help children to understand how their behaviour can affect others?

- **Introducing the concept of individual liberty:** Do you help children to develop a positive sense of themselves and the confidence to do new things?

- **Introducing mutual respect and tolerance:** Do you help children to find out more about other cultures, in an inclusive and tolerant atmosphere?

- **Do you actively challenge**:
  o   intolerance of other faiths, cultures and races;
  o   gender stereotypes and routine segregation of boys and girls, with no educational purpose;
  o   isolation of children from the wider community;
  o   any behaviour by staff, parents or children which is not in line with the British values outlined above?

The Early Years Pupil Premium

The Early Years Pupil Premium (EYPP) was introduced in April 2015 to address another fundamental equality issue: children from more advantaged backgrounds achieve much better levels of development by the end of the EYFS than those from disadvantaged backgrounds. The gap between richer and poorer children is a particular problem in the English education system – it is much worse here than in countries like Canada or Finland, for example. This issue has particularly concerned Her Majesty's former Chief Inspector of Schools, Sir Michael Wilshaw, and, as a result, Ofsted is very focussed on the use of the EYPP. If you have eligible children, the impact of the EYPP will be specifically checked and reported on by Ofsted as part of their inspection.

At the time of writing, the EYPP amounted to 53 pence per hour for each eligible child: it is a small amount of money. Nevertheless, because it is public money provided to early years settings for a specific purpose, Ofsted will hold you clearly to account for how you spent it and what its impact was. There is plenty of very helpful guidance available online to help you decide how best to spend the funding, for example:

- Early Education - www.early-education.org.uk/eypp.

- Early Years Toolkit - https://educationendowmentfoundation.org.uk/evidence/early-years-toolkit.

- Foundation Years - www.foundationyears.org.uk/category/eypp.

Whilst the decision on how to spend the EYPP will depend on the particular circumstances of your setting, it is important that you begin with a focus on how things are. As well as looking at eligible children overall, focus on each child as an individual. What were the starting points of your eligible children, and how much progress are they making compared to other children? Next, you need to consider whether there are any barriers to progress and whether you can use the funding to help overcome those barriers. For example, at Sheringham Nursery School there was a group of eligible children whose attendance was poor, so we invested some of the EYPP into working directly with those families to boost attendance. We were mindful that research carried out in the London Borough of Merton showed that the single strongest predictor of poor development by the end of the EYFS was poor attendance.

Throughout your cycle of actions, you should be evaluating all the time (Figure 5.2). If you invest your funding in a particular area and then discover at the end of the year that it has not helped the eligible children, it will be too late to do anything – and those children will not have that year again.

Governance

If you are part of a school, then Ofsted will consider the impact of governance when they judge the quality of leadership and management. This will be a whole-school issue, so it is only considered briefly here.

Firstly, you will need to ensure that governors have an accurate understanding of the strengths and weaknesses of your EYFS provision. This understanding will have been gained through processes of dialogue, support and challenge. So, your

Figure 5.2 A suggested process for implementing the EYPP

Ofsted inspector will want to see how you report to the governing body on the effectiveness of your provision. Do governors have the opportunity to undertake Learning Walks or other activities to supplement their knowledge of the provision? Is there evidence that they support, but also challenge you where necessary? Governors will take a view, based on the reports they receive from the school, on the overall quality of the EYFS and it will be important to check that they understand what the judgements mean. If you consider your EYFS practice to be Good, it is important to check that your governors – especially the chair, and the EYFS governor if you have one – can talk about what Good means, and what evidence they have to back up their views. So, when you report to governors, make sure you make plenty of references to the section of the Ofsted handbook about the EYFS.

Other documentation

The section above outlines all the things which you *must* do to fulfil your leadership and management responsibilities. Many of these requirements are set out in law, and you risk being judged Inadequate if you do not comply with them. You should be prepared for your Ofsted inspector to ask to see documentation which relates to these areas:

- Your staff deployment plan, which should be consistent with the ratio and qualification requirements set out in the EYFS Statutory Framework.

- Your recruitment records, showing how you make safer recruitment decisions and prevent unsuitable people from working with your young children through interviewing, following up references and using the DBS.

- Records of staff training for safeguarding practice and procedures, showing that all staff have been appropriately trained.

- Records of any complaints received and how these have been managed.

Ofsted expectations for leadership and management

In addition to the legal requirements explained above, Ofsted will expect to see your leadership and management systems in the following areas. The key question for your inspector will be: what is the *impact* of these systems? How do they ensure that every child has a positive experience in your provision?

Planning and assessment documents

The inspection of your leadership and management will include scrutinising a sample of your planning and assessment documents. At one time, the evaluation of this aspect seemed to have a rather disproportionate effect on inspection judgements, and this resulted in lots of rumours about the sort of documents Ofsted expected to see, and the quantity. Early years settings across the sectors felt obliged to produce long and hugely detailed documents to satisfy Ofsted's demands.

Ofsted now state clearly that they do not need to see individual lesson plans (which would include 'session' plans for the early years). They do not take a view about how planning should be set out or how much detail it should include. A similar line is taken about assessment. There is now only one question which concerns Ofsted: are your planning and assessment documents *effective*? In other words, do they help practitioners as they work with children, toddlers and babies, to offer a stimulating environment, appropriate routines, and opportunities for children to develop and learn from their different starting points? It is up to each school and setting to decide how to achieve this.

Induction, training and continuous professional development

As I argued in Part 1, your approach to the support and professional development of your team is fundamental to the quality of your provision. The approaches outlined earlier, adapted to your own specific circumstances, will provide you with the type of evidence that your inspector may ask to see. So, you will need to consider and to show evidence of how well your induction processes support new members of the team. Are you diligent about making sure all new team members understand your safeguarding policy and procedures, and your behaviour policy? How you help them to offer the care and teaching which is in line with your ethos? How do you identify whether a new member of staff needs extra help to reach the standards you expect, and how do you evaluate the impact of the support you offer?

If your setting includes students and trainees, you will need to demonstrate that you are supporting their development and giving them the practical help and encouragement they need to develop. This is likely to include having named mentors, a cycle of mentor meetings and systematic observations, together with time for reflection and identification of the next steps for development. It is important to remember that the key focus must always be on the wellbeing, safety, care and education of the children: if the actions of students and trainees are undermining that, then you need to put the children first and liaise with the college, university or training provider about withdrawing the person concerned from your provision either temporarily, until they can meet minimum standards, or permanently.

Where you include volunteers, you will want to follow the same principles as you do for students and trainees, although with a 'lighter touch'.

If you are able to show that your ongoing cycle of induction, support and continuous professional development has a positive impact on the quality of care and teaching, and the outcomes for the children, then Ofsted will see this as a significant strength.

Ethos and vision

Ofsted consider that leaders and managers should demonstrate 'ambitious vision' and 'high expectations'. As I argued in the first part of this book, building a strong team and setting out your ethos and your vision are essential to success. For the specific purposes of inspection, I would argue that it will be not be helpful to set this out in 'flowery language' and through a long and complex document about your aims and values. As I suggested in Part 1, a clear statement which avoids jargon and high theory can state clearly what you want to achieve as a team for the children and their families.

Organising your self-evaluation

Ofsted have told schools that they do not 'require self-evaluation to be provided in a specific format. Any assessment that is provided should be part of the school's business processes and not generated solely for inspection purposes'. As a result, they do not offer a suggested format for self-evaluation. Somewhat confusingly, they *do* provide a suggested format for early years settings which are not schools. You can either complete this online, in which case your inspector can read it before their arrival, or you can download it and fill in a hard-copy. Contrary to what Ofsted say to schools, they actively encourage other early years settings to use their form.

In practice, if you are the EYFS leader in a school, then you will need to follow your whole-school approach to self-evaluation. But you might find the Ofsted form helpful just to make sure that what you are doing is comprehensive and considers all the different aspects of the Common Inspection Framework as it applies to the early years. If you are a setting, whilst you are allowed to use whatever form of self-evaluation you like, it will be more straightforward and less risky to take the easy route and use the form and guidance which Ofsted have published online here: www.gov.uk/government/publications/early-years-online-self-evaluation-form-sef-and-guidance-for-providers-delivering-the-early-years-foundation-stage.

Reflection point

Your first priority is to make sure that you meet all the requirements and expectations set out above.

Evaluating your leadership and management is about *impact*. For that reason, you need to wait until you have self-evaluated all the other areas first, and then return to this one. Only in very specific circumstances could your leadership and management be evaluated at a higher level than, say, personal development, behaviour and welfare, or teaching, learning and assessment. You might be able to show that your leadership is so effective that you are making rapid improvements in all areas. Then, even though some areas still Require Improvement, your leadership could be Good.

Thinking about the broad phases of development outlined in Part 1:

Table 5.1

Phase one: Practice which works for you.	Your leadership and management will most likely be Good once you have consolidated this phase. At earlier stages, you will probably Require Improvement.
Phase two: Practice which works for you, and is consistent with the research and evidence base.	Your leadership and management will most likely be Good and heading towards Outstanding.
Phase three: Developing leading-edge practice.	Your leadership and management will most likely be Outstanding.

6

The Common Inspection Framework

Quality of teaching, learning and assessment

Introduction

Quality of teaching, learning and assessment is another area where Ofsted's approach has changed significantly with the Common Inspection Framework. Firstly, if you are a setting working with babies and children before the age of two years, it may seem surprising that Ofsted will be looking at your 'teaching'. After all, what does 'teaching' a six-month-old mean? In recent years, Ofsted have been quite confrontational in their stance towards the early years world, insisting on the language of teaching and education. There are many, legitimate concerns about the tone they have struck. However, it *is* possible to work with this framework, without compromising on your offer of warm, loving care for babies and young toddlers.

Secondly, the addition of 'assessment' to the title of this section of the framework is significant. The emphasis is very much on whether the teaching observed is appropriate for the children involved. So, your Ofsted inspector will want to see that the children's previous learning has been assessed and taken into account, and will want to see how children at different stages of development are being helped to make progress. There have been numerous myths over the years about what Ofsted wanted to see when they observed a session or a lesson, in terms of how the children were organised, how ideas were introduced, etc. There were even books and courses – mostly aimed at teachers working with older children – with titles like *The Perfect Ofsted Lesson* (Beere, 2010). But there is no 'perfect' Ofsted lesson any more, only teaching which is effective (or not) for the particular children you work with.

In this chapter, 'assessment' is considered to be the information which practitioners use to make sure their teaching is well-matched to the individual learning and care needs of the children. Those assessments may arise from written observations and be recorded, or they may arise from team discussions about the children, like a quick review meeting at the end of the day. Assessment does not need to mean lots of bureaucracy, taking of photos on your tablet, or writing information down. The use of assessment to monitor children's progress is considered in Chapter 8.

As already discussed, Ofsted are explicit that they do not favour any one style of teaching: their only concern is whether teaching is effective in ensuring that children make strong and sustained progress from their starting points. For the same reason, Ofsted will not grade the teaching they see. If you have been observed and then you ask for feedback from your Ofsted inspector, you will no longer be told whether your teaching is Outstanding, Good, Requiring Improvement or Inadequate. Instead, the discussion will focus on what the inspector observed was effective in helping children to learn, and what was observed to be ineffective. You will have professional dialogue about your work, but you will not go away with a grade. I would argue that this is a much more grown up way for the inspectorate to engage with practitioners.

But, for the early years, Ofsted's neutrality about styles of teaching is a little more complicated. The EYFS Statutory Framework specifies particular approaches to teaching and learning. Because these approaches are set out in law, Ofsted *will* check for them. The framework requires that: 'each area of learning and development must be implemented through planned, purposeful play and through a mix of adult-led and child-initiated activity'. Practitioners must plan for children's learning both indoors and outdoors. The framework states that: 'play is essential for children's development' and sets out three Characteristics of Effective Learning:

1. Playing and Exploring.
2. Active Learning.
3. Creating and Thinking Critically.

So, you will need to show and have evidence that your approach to teaching and care in the EYFS is consistent with the Statutory Framework. Drawing on this, Ofsted include a very useful definition of what they mean by early years 'teaching' in both the *Early Years* (2015e) and the *School Inspection* (2015d) handbooks:

> Teaching should not be taken to imply a 'top-down' or formal way of working. It is a broad term that covers the many different ways in which adults help young children learn. It includes their interactions with children during planned and child-initiated play and activities: communicating and modelling

language, showing, explaining, demonstrating, exploring ideas, encouraging, questioning, recalling, providing a narrative for what they are doing, facilitating and setting challenges. It takes account of the equipment adults provide and the attention given to the physical environment, as well as the structure and routines of the day that establish expectations. Integral to teaching is how practitioners assess what children know, understand and can do, as well as taking account of their interests and dispositions to learn (Characteristics of Effective Learning), and how practitioners use this information to plan children's next steps in learning and monitor their progress.

It is worth remembering that there is a very important distinction between your role as a leader and a manager, and Ofsted's role as the inspectorate. You are in charge of teaching and learning, not Ofsted. As a leader, you will want to work with your team to develop an agreed approach to teaching and learning, informed by your experience of what works in your context, expressing your principles and values, and drawing on research evidence. It is perfectly appropriate for you to look for those features of teaching and learning when you are observing practice. If you want to see play-based learning, you could look for the 12 features of play proposed by Tina Bruce (2015). The success of your provision will depend to a large degree on how you have developed a coherent approach with your team, how you support and challenge colleagues when they fall short of what is expected, and how well you monitor outcomes to check that what you are doing is effective and appropriate.

Because the aim of this book is to support you to prepare for your inspection, the sections below do not constitute a guide to effective care, teaching and learning in the EYFS. There are plenty of excellent books for you to turn to for that, for example:

- Tina Bruce (2004) *Developing Learning in Early Childhood (Zero to Eight)*. London: SAGE.

- Vicky Hutchin (2012) *The EYFS: A Practical Guide for Students and Professionals*. London: Hodder.

- Nancy Stewart (2011) *How Children Learn: The Characteristics of Effective Early Learning*. London: Early Education.

Instead, I am offering suggestions about how you can generate and manage useful information about the quality of teaching, learning and assessment. You can use this information for two purposes: to monitor and improve your provision, and as evidence for Ofsted to support your self-evaluation. Good-quality information will enable you to make an accurate self-evaluation, and this in turn will mean that the Ofsted inspection will largely be a validation of what you are doing. It is also important for you to have good evidence of how you monitor the quality of teaching over time, because this will mean that if some of the team have a bad day when Ofsted are in, you can make a strong case for what the quality of teaching usually looks like, and you can back this up with evidence about its impact over time with evidence about the children's progress from their starting point. This is discussed in more detail in Chapter 8.

But more fundamentally, regularly monitoring the quality of teaching is important because it enables you to improve teaching over time. An effective early years setting is always looking to improve, no matter how good it is.

An effective monitoring process will include accurate observation of practice, followed by professional dialogue focussed on improvement. It is important to build up staff confidence about being observed, so that you can do this regularly and in a way which benefits individuals rather than leading them to think they are constantly under surveillance and scrutiny. The message that monitoring takes place to improve practice and to inform future plans for continuous professional development can be very helpful.

A good approach to improving accuracy is to involve a second person. This means that after the observation, you can discuss what you saw together, challenge each other and draw attention to things which may have been missed. It is useful to bring people in from outside your own organisation as often as you can – practitioners from other schools and settings, for example, or consultants. That way, you can challenge your assumptions and you can test out whether your standards and expectations are appropriately geared – or whether you expect too much, or too little. It is helpful to attend regular training, too, to keep your skills sharp and up to date.

As discussed in Part 1, staff can also be encouraged to undertake peer observations, observing and feeding back to each other in order to build a shared understanding of effective teaching. This approach can encourage an open culture where the focus is on improving the children's experience.

Table 6.1 is an example of the observation format which can be used either to observe a specific practitioner, or an area (a room or the outdoors), or an area of work (displays, children's Special Books). In this case, the provision in Rainbow Room for children aged three and four years old was the focus for observation. The table lists aspects to observe on the left-hand side as a memory aid: there is no expectation that all of these points should be documented on the right-hand side.

Table 6.1

Names: Of teacher/room leader and staff undertaking observation.	Michele observing Razia, Alex, Muhammad and Denise (with Leila, L2 student) in Rainbow Room.
Context: Date, time, place and children involved.	10.20 a.m., adults supporting child-initiated play with Alex guiding learning in woodwork area and Razia in snack area.
Principles and values observed in action: ● Equality. ● Inclusion. ● Respect for the Child.	Inclusion: exemplary practice in inclusion of Jamal at snack table (he was given the chance to spread his toast, and as he could not manage, Razia did hand-over-hand modelling) and at the mark-making table where Denise encouraged him over a long period of time to cut and tear paper. Staff at all times showed their respect for children, listening attentively and encouraging their efforts. Boys and girls encouraged to access all learning (e.g. girls at woodwork table).

Characteristics of Effective Learning observed: • Playing and Exploring. • Active Learning. • Creating and Thinking Critically. Comment on Emotional Warmth and Quality of Care. Comment on children's Spiritual, Moral, Social and Cultural Development.	There were multiple examples of playing and exploring and active learning, e.g. boy exploring thick paint with rolling pins on own; two girls playing with elephants and talking together; block play by a girl over 15 minutes. Snack-promoted active learning – making choices, spreading, putting plates in sink when finished with. Children were creating with blocks and in the woodwork area. Support for thinking critically was observed from Muhammad in block play: 'I can put my hand through … can you fit the block in that space?' – 'Perhaps it's slightly shorter,' etc. Alex encouraged a child to look over the design he was making with pieces of wood and the glue gun, so he decided to add some more items and placed them carefully before sticking them down. Children's social development was exceptionally well promoted by staff who encouraged children to share, listen to each other, and co-operate in their play.
Evidence of children making progress in their learning: • Concepts. • Attitudes. • Skills.	Progress observed: Jamal in tearing, cutting and spreading; children learnt to use the glue gun safely; Muhammad supported learning about spaces and solving problems with blocks; Denise consistently encouraged good attitudes to learning and bouncing back from problems 'keep trying' – 'nearly there' – 'you're working hard on that'.
Evidence of how well teaching supports the learning of children at different ages, levels of development, and with special educational needs.	Teaching and learning was highly effective – children with SEN making good progress with skills and developing attention; children deeply engaged in high-level woodwork and block play; snack table supported each child at their own level, from independent choosing, spreading and washing up, to guided spreading.
Summary: What is enabling children's learning?	• Very calm and purposeful. • Very good quality of interactions with children to extend their language and learning. • Challenging activities, e.g. woodwork. • Excellent support for children with SEN. • Teaching well matched to different levels of development.
Summary: What is holding back children's learning?	• Leila the student on placement makes an important contribution but was not always observed to be supporting children as effectively, e.g. wanting a child to finish block play and move onto another activity, when the child was very absorbed in what she was doing.
Post-observation dialogue: Denise explained that Leila needed to start to take more responsibility for activities, as required for her course. After further discussion, we agreed that the balance was not quite right between her needs as a trainee and the children's entitlement to the best quality of early education.	

(Continued)

Table 6.1   (Continued)

Muhammad explained how block play was developing over time and shared several observations showing these developments – the quality of play observed in the session was consistent with the quality of play over a longer time period. The children are making strong progress, e.g. engaged for longer periods of time, and solving more complex problems.
Outcomes/next steps (maximum of three):
The team agreed that Leila needed a higher level of supervision, with all staff being aware of her level/competency so that they can model, support or intervene as appropriate.

Where practice is not so positive, it is even more important to focus sharply on what is effective in promoting children's learning, and what is holding them back. Table 6.2 gives an example of a 20-minute observation in a two-year-olds' room. The observer has drawn on Ofsted's (2015d) useful guidance in the *School Inspection Handbook* on 'inspecting provision for two-year-olds'.

Table 6.2

Names: Of teacher/room leader and staff undertaking observation.	Rabia observing Fatima and Annette working with a small group of two-year-olds.
Context: Date, time, place and children involved.	1.30–1.50 p.m. This is an adult-guided activity at the circular table involving four children, Rashid, Billy, Faith (new to the room) and Adam (special needs – delayed communication).
Principles and values observed in action: • Equality. • Inclusion. • Respect for the Child.	Staff were patient and attentive at the start of the activity, meaning children were able to express their ideas. When Adam could not express what he wanted, staff missed his non-verbal cues. This led to Adam having a tantrum, and when he was sent away, he missed out on the opportunities given to the other children and he continued to be angry and upset for some time without anyone helping or comforting him. His wellbeing and PSED were not being supported.
Characteristics of Effective Learning observed: • Playing and Exploring. • Active Learning. • Creating and Thinking Critically.	The children were eager to come over at the start to the table, which was draped with beautiful, patterned cloth and had a big book, *Handa's Surprise*, at the centre. The four children listened attentively to the story at first and were given time to make their own comments. Rashid – 'we got basket at home' Billy – 'put head!'

Comment on Emotional Warmth and Quality of Care. Comment on children's Spiritual, Moral, Social and Cultural Development.	Faith had been taken to the table by her mum and then looked a bit lost and upset when her mum left. Not clear who Faith's key person is, no-one seemed especially to comfort her. She looked around the room most of the time and did not talk during the activity. After the book was finished, the practitioners gave each child a colour photocopy of the fruits to stick on a photocopy of a basket. Rashid said, 'My mum eats avocado, I don't like it,' but no one replied and because there was no real avocado to try, the other children could not talk about or experience this. Adam's scissors were caked with old glue and he could not cut with them. He may have been communicating that he needed help by banging them on the table. The scissors were taken off him and when he shouted he was sent away from the table. Faith then began to cry and the activity was quickly brought to an end.
Evidence of children making progress in their learning: • Concepts. • Attitudes. • Skills.	According to the plan and to what the practitioners said, the activity was planned because *Handa's Surprise* is a favourite book of Rashid's. The planning did not identify what learning might arise from building on Rashid's interest. The activity did not help children to develop their cutting skills because some scissors had old glue over them, and, even where scissors were sharp it was too difficult to cut round the photocopied shapes and children resorted to tearing.
Evidence of how well teaching supports the learning of children at different ages, levels of development, and with special educational needs.	No evidence was seen to suggest that the activity was adapted to meet Adam's special needs.
Summary: What is enabling children's learning?	• Fatima and Annette show kindness to the children and give them time to talk. • They notice children's interests. • The room was organised so that the circular table was in a quiet corner to enable the children to listen and watch.
Summary: what is holding back children's learning?	• Planning focusses on finding children's interests and then 'extending' them without thinking through how the activity will help children's development. • Missing Adam's non-verbal cues and sending him away prevented him from taking part and learning, and from developing socially.

(Continued)

Table 6.2 (Continued)

	• Children did not talk about the different fruit: planning and resourcing were ineffective. • Lack of attention at times to care needs, e.g. Faith did not have support from her key person.

Post-observation dialogue:

Fatima and Annette said they were very upset about this observation. Rabia explained that she had focussed on seeing the responses of the children. She understands that Fatima and Annette are very caring and want the best for the children. However, this session was ineffective and has highlighted support and CPD needs for the team around the key person approach, planning, and using high-quality resources to promote children's learning and communication. Fatima and Annette agreed that reading the book and tasting different fruit would have been more enjoyable for the young children and would have promoted more learning and talking.

Outcomes/next steps (maximum of three)

• Rabia will look at the team's CPD needs and she will provide training/support over the next three months focussed on the key person approach, planning and using high-quality resources to promote children's learning and communication. Each session of team CPD will make clear expectations of improved practice and Rabia will then check that this is being implemented.
• Fatima and Annette will replan this activity using real fruit for the children to taste and talk about.
• Fatima and Annette will consistently implement the strategies for Adam as advised by speech and language therapy.

The enabling environment

As stated above, the EYFS Statutory Framework requires practitioners to plan for children's learning both indoors and out, and emphasises the role of the enabling environment in helping children to learn – as well as adult care, support, interaction and teaching. Ofsted (2015d and 2015e) describe this as: 'the equipment adults provide and the attention given to the physical environment, as well as the structure and routines of the day that establish expectations' in their definition of early years teaching.

The Environmental Rating Scales (ITERS-R, ECERS-3 and ECERS-E) are, I would argue, the most comprehensive tools which you can use to evaluate the quality of your provision in these areas, and to inform an action plan to make improvements where necessary. This will then provide evidence of the improvements you have made, both for your own purposes, and for Ofsted.

The ITERS-R scales are suitable for provision for children up to the age of three, and the ECERS-3 and ECERS-E scales are suitable for nursery and reception provision for older children in the EYFS. The scales are very robust, and the EPPE Project demonstrated the association between high scores (4 and above) and good outcomes for children (Sylva et al., 2010).

The best approach to using the scales is to invite a trained, independent assessor to visit your setting and audit its quality. Many local authority teams have trained assessors, and the national organisation A Plus Education (www. aplus-education.co.uk) can also undertake this work.

The value of the scales lies in their rigour, helping you to identify areas of quality, and areas which need to change. The evidence from the audits, together with your action plan to make improvements, can enable you to be on the front foot with Ofsted, so that your inspection mostly validates accurate judgements you have already made. It can also be very helpful if things do not go well on the day – you can show evidence that an area of provision that was not so good on the day, is effective and is improving over time.

As with all tools, you will need to apply professional judgement. It is possible that because of the nature of your premises, some environment scores will never be as high – in which case, make a note about the restrictions in your premises and explain how you are doing the best you can to overcome the limitations.

The Characteristics of Effective Learning

One of the principal ways that Ofsted will judge the quality of teaching, learning and assessment is by looking for evidence of children showing the Characteristics of Effective Learning (CEL):

- Playing and Exploring - engagement.

- Active Learning - motivation.

- Creating and Thinking Critically - thinking.

These are helpfully explained in the non-statutory guidance to the EYFS, *Development Matters* (Early Education, 2012: 4–6). Each 'characteristic' is broken down into four examples of the sorts of learning behaviour you might see, with sections on how adults and how the environment can help this learning. It is unfortunate when practitioners who use *Development Matters* flip quickly over the opening pages and go straight into the descriptions of children's learning at different ages and stages. The EYFS is carefully structured the other way round: it puts its main emphasis on *how* children learn, and how adults and the learning environment can help children. It then prioritises the three Prime Areas of learning (Personal, Social and Emotional Development, Communication and Language, and Physical Development) which are viewed as essential to *all* learning across the EYFS. This does not mean that children learn the Prime Areas first, and then the specific ones next: rather, the specific areas depend on the Prime Areas. To take one example, children are not going to learn to write, if there is not a strong focus on their communication. If you cannot yet speak a sentence (or communicate one in sign language), then you are not going to be able to think one up and write it. Similarly, writing depends on physical development: if you cannot use your arm, hand and finger muscles together to manipulate a pencil or pen, you are not going to be able to form any letters.

In my experience, many EYFS settings make appropriate provision for children's playing and exploring. This depends on giving children the space, time, equipment and adult support to enable them to develop their play over time, and to explore a range of different experiences. The ECERS-3 and ITERS-R tools are an excellent way of assessing the quality of your provision in these areas.

The second area of the CEL is a little trickier. There is often an appropriate focus in EYFS settings on children's active learning, which includes prioritising uninterrupted periods of time so that children can get deeply involved in what they are doing rather than having to stop what they are doing every ten minutes for circle time, assembly, snack, etc. The Leuven scales, which are used in the Effective Early Learning Programme (Pascal and Bertram, 1997) are a good tool to use to check how involved children are in their learning and the extent to which they show energy and persistence. The Active Learning strand of the CEL also focusses on developing children's self-motivation in their learning. This means that you would expect to see children showing the motivation to take on challenges in their learning. The important work of the educational researcher Carol Dweck (2006) suggests that this motivation can be undermined by practitioners offering children too much praise: everything from constant 'well dones' to the stickers and charts that exist to reward children's efforts. Dweck's research suggests that far from building up a child's self-esteem, praise which focusses on achievement rather than on effort might actually have a negative effect. It results in children doing things in order to be praised. Children may take on easier tasks which they think they will get right, and therefore win praise for, rather than try harder things which may go wrong and therefore not result in a 'well done' or a sticker on the chart.

The third area of the CEL, Creating and Thinking Critically, is perhaps the most challenging. This focusses on provision and teaching which helps children to develop their ways of thinking and to become more aware of how they go about their learning (known as their 'metacognition'). Research evidence, especially from the EPPE Project, suggests that these features are found in highly effective early years settings. *Development Matters* (Early Education, 2012) refers to the development of 'a learning community which focusses on **how** and not just what we are learning'. Practitioners who support children in this area can often capitalise on children's immediate interests in a way which promotes extended discussion and exploration.

A useful tool which will help you to evaluate and develop the quality of your provision in this area is the *Sustained Shared Thinking and Emotional Well-Being (SSTEW) Scale for 2–5-Year-Olds Provision* (Siraj et al., 2015)

Table 6.3 gives an example of effective practice in this area, from a session observation in a reception class. Because the observer wants to capture the 'feel' of this exemplary teaching, she has mostly ignored the prompts on the pro forma.

Table 6.3

Names: Of teacher/room leader and staff undertaking observation.	Karen observing Penna.
Context: Date, time, place and children involved.	9–9.20 a.m. in the main playground. Four boys (Chris, Simon, Kamal, Rob) are with Penna. Planning – the boys are fascinated by the new bikes, so they have a short time out in the school playground without the distraction of other children, rather than using the reception garden. There is a selection of bikes and trikes.
Principles and values observed in action: • Equality. • Inclusion. • Respect for the Child. **Characteristics of Effective Learning observed:** • Playing and Exploring. • Active Learning. • Creating and Thinking Critically. Comment on Emotional Warmth and Quality of Care. Comment on children's Spiritual, Moral, Social and Cultural Development. **Evidence of children making progress in their learning** • Concepts. • Attitudes. • Skills. **Evidence of how well teaching supports the learning of children at different ages, levels of development, and with special educational needs.**	Penna: 'Wow look at the new bikes, I bet they're fast.' Chris: 'Yeah watch' (speeds off on metal balance bike, turns and comes back). Penna: 'How come they're so fast?' Simon: 'Because they're new.' Penna: 'But the trikes are new, too, but I don't think they're so fast.' Simon: 'But they got little wheels.' Penna: 'OK, so do big wheels go faster than little wheels?' Kamal: 'Yeah.' Penna: 'OK, that's interesting, I wonder how we could find out more?' Kamal: 'Let's do a race.' Penna lines up a trike, two metal balance bikes and a pedal bike. Everyone wants a metal balance bike but Penna supports the children by saying she needs their help for a race, she needs a rider for every bike. The race is to the fence and back. After the race: Penna: 'OK, so what happened?' Rob: 'I came first …' Penna: 'Yes, you did, let's look at your wheels then to see if they are the biggest.' Children look at the wheels. Chris: 'Those wheels are the same size as Kamal's.' Rob: 'I think you need a bigger person [thinks] but Chris is bigger than me, I think he came last.' Chris: 'Yeah, but I had to do the pedals and they're hard and I fell over, that wasn't fair.'

(Continued)

Table 6.3 (Continued)

	Rob: 'The pedals make you slower!' Simon: 'But my mum has pedals on her bike and she's *really* fast ...'
Summary: What is enabling children's learning?	• Children are encouraged to come up with their own ideas and explore them (sustained shared thinking). • Children are given motivating opportunities to develop the Characteristics of Effective Learning, and to develop their scientific thinking. • Careful planning – builds well on previous observations/assessments and interests to support children in making strong progress in their reasoning and scientific thinking. • Children are flourishing – fascination, enjoyment, creative thinking.
Summary: What is holding back children's learning?	• NA.

Post-observation dialogue:

Penna initially felt that this had not been fully effective because the children had not developed their thinking about 'fair tests'. Karen felt that the focus on sustained and creative thinking was more appropriate and that Penna had done the right thing by focussing on and developing the children's responses, rather than sticking rigidly to a plan.

Outcomes/next steps (maximum of three):

- Karen will share this observation with the whole team to celebrate highly effective practice.
- Karen will support the team in thinking about those boys whose speaking is assessed as being much lower than girls – do they need more motivating contexts like this to make stronger development?
- Penna will informally support and encourage the rest of the team to develop extended conversations with children like these.

Reflection point

These questions may help you to consider the effectiveness of the steps you are taking to improve the quality of teaching, learning and assessment:

- Do you use appropriate tools for self-evaluation, so you know where to focus your CPD and leadership in order to improve teaching?

- Do you balance your role in monitoring quality, with your role in improving practice through modelling, coaching and curriculum development? Lots of management and monitoring will not, in itself, make anything better.

- Does all your monitoring result in professional dialogue, with a focus on children's learning and care? Do you follow up action points regularly, and give staff the support and training they need to achieve them?

- Do you bring in others to observe with you (e.g. other experienced leaders, specialist consultants, practitioners who are also trained Ofsted inspectors) in order to help you sharpen your observation skills and challenge your thinking?

Thinking about the broad phases of development outlined in Part 1:

Table 6.4

Phase one: Practice which works for you.	You will need to consolidate this phase so that your teaching, learning and assessment will be Good. At earlier stages, you will probably Require Improvement. Your focus will be on making sure that everyone in the team is consistent in the 'basics' (e.g. in a nursery class, supporting children's Personal, Social and Emotional Development, Physical Development and early Communication, and encouraging their playing, exploring and active learning). You will keep new innovations and developments to a minimum until you are achieving this consistently.
Phase two: Practice which works for you, and is consistent with the research and evidence base.	Your teaching, learning and assessment will be consistently Good. You will be introducing tools like the SSTEW scale to apply research findings in order to develop some areas of highly effective practice.
Phase three: Developing leading-edge practice.	You will be considering research like the EPPSE project findings and using tools like the SSTEW scale regularly. You will be adapting these tools and research findings in the light of the very specific characteristics of your children and local context. Your teaching, learning and assessment will most likely be Outstanding.

7

The Common Inspection Framework

Personal development, behaviour and welfare

Introduction

There is a longstanding view that early years education has to be understood as being integrated with care. For all practitioners across the EYFS, being able to offer high-quality care is essential if children are to have an appropriate experience, whether we are focussed on ensuring supportive feeding, nappy-changing and sleep routines for babies, or on settling in four-year-olds who are new to reception. All the young children in the early years need warm and consistent care, and the Statutory Framework requires that this is underpinned by a key person system.

So, this third section of the Ofsted framework is particularly important when considering the EYFS. It is important to note that the emphasis has changed in this area.

Ofsted now report separately on behaviour, and about personal development and welfare – whereas they used to be considered together. This is intended to give parents a clearer view of how good behaviour is in schools and settings. I would argue that disentangling these two aspects is particularly difficult in the EYFS. It might make more sense in the case of older children, where there might be good practice in promoting their welfare, but behaviour might not be so good because there is constant low-level disruption in lessons. But young children in the EYFS are at the early stages of learning about how to manage their emotions, get on with others, and learn in a group: it all overlaps.

Attendance

The question of attendance and punctuality is another tricky area in the EYFS. If you are running a setting where parents are paying for childcare, which includes early education, then the times and the rate of attendance are really down to the parent and not you!

If children are accessing their free entitlement at two, three or four years old, or in reception, then late arrival will mean that they are missing out on educational opportunities compared to their peers. So, you will need to think about how you challenge regular lateness in a firm but polite way. If lateness continues, then you will need to think about what else you might need to do to help improve timekeeping. Do families need some advice on getting ready in good time, which you might be able to give them? Would it help to phone an hour before nursery starts? Could you refer to your local Children's Centre for family support? It is likely that children who are regularly late will be affected by other aspects of disorganised family life – so, offering early help is a good idea.

In schools, attendance levels in the EYFS are very likely to be lower than they are for children in Key Stage One or Two. In an early years provision, babies and young children are encountering lots of new germs which their immune systems are not yet ready to deal with – so coughs, colds and tummy bugs will be rife. The important thing is to show that you have good systems to pick up where children's attendance is poor, and that you take effective action to improve attendance. For example, you need to distinguish between the child who has a week off with flu, and the child who is off a day a week throughout the term for different reasons. Explaining the importance of good attendance to parents is vital, especially if they take the view that this phase of education doesn't matter as the children are so young, so missing days here and there will not be a problem.

Attendance also links to safeguarding. If you are not seeing a child regularly, where are they? How do you know if they are safe and well? Children who are sick expectedly often, may be neglected children: perhaps they are not kept warm enough, or are not eating well, or do not have enough sleep? You will need to use your professional judgement in all these areas and, where appropriate, may need to bring in extra help or make a safeguarding referral.

Ultimately, attendance is not compulsory in the early years until the term after a child's fifth birthday, so there are no sanctions for poor attendance. To handle the discussion of attendance well with your Ofsted inspector, explain all the different things you do to maximise attendance, and give examples of their impact (for example, the child whose attendance improves during the year as a result of your actions). If there is a suggestion that attendance will affect your judgement, ask what other steps the inspector would advise you to take to improve attendance further. If there are no suggested further steps, then ask whether it is fair for this to affect your outcome, given that you are following every possible strategy, and attendance is not compulsory.

Safety, welfare and safeguarding

As previously discussed in the Safeguarding section of Chapter 5, Ofsted will want to see that you follow all the relevant procedures, comply with all the relevant legislation, *and* that your actions have positive impact. Your inspector will want to evaluate the experience of children where there has been a referral to the local authority for safeguarding reasons. This will include wanting to see how the referral was made, how it was followed up, and what the outcomes have been for the child.

The welfare of children with medical and special educational needs or disabilities

Ofsted will also check that children with specific needs are being kept safe and well. If children need medication, then you must show that you are meeting the requirements set out in the EYFS Statutory Framework. Every dose must be recorded, signed for by the person giving the medication, and counter-signed by the parent. It is, of course, vital that the right dose is given and that if a mistake is made through human error this is immediately acted on by seeking medical advice and informing the parent. Some children with special educational needs and disabilities will also have specific care and welfare needs and you will need to show how you are meeting these needs. For example, for a visually impaired child, you will need to take steps to reduce the danger of the child bumping into equipment or fall-ing over, such as by using carefully contrasting colours and arranging the furniture and outdoor equipment with care, as advised by a specialist. If children are using wheelchairs or standing frames, there will need to be enough space for them to navigate the areas, and play experiences will need to be presented at the right height for them. It will also be very important that you are positive about diversity and disability through your resources, displays and teaching.

Providing case studies

Your Ofsted inspector may ask to see a small sample of case studies about the individual children or groups outlined above. However, it is useful to know that there is no expectation or requirement about how these should be presented, and you definitely should not find yourself undertaking a burdensome task that takes hours to complete. A very simple, one-page format would be perfectly adequate to explain situations like those outlined in the examples above. Where you have been working in partnership, ask others to contribute a sentence or two. For example, if you have been supported by an area SENCO, ask them for a comment on the adaptations you have made and their impact. Include the parent's voice. You should also think about how the child's voice might be included, either through what they say, or by capturing their response to the opportunities and help you have provided.

These types of case studies can also help with your self-evaluation, especially if you think through what you have learnt and what you would do differently and better next time.

Evaluating your effectiveness

Whilst Ofsted call this area 'personal development, behaviour and welfare', I would argue that in the early years – and in keeping with the EYFS Statutory Framework – it makes more sense to think about this slightly differently. I would prefer to consider the quality of care, the promotion of positive behaviour, and children's progress in their Personal, Social and Emotional Development.

The EYFS Statutory Framework requires that care should be organised around the key person approach. This approach involves each child having an allocated key person, whose role is to build a close relationship with that child, and also with the child's parents. The key person approach is *not* primarily about organising who is in charge of each child's observations or records. It is based on the theory that young children in early years settings need to have a special relationship, beginning with the phase of settling in, in order that they can feel emotionally safe and secure and not just be one of a big group of children.

A key person is:

- A named member of staff who has more contact than others with the child.

- Someone to build a relationship with the child and parents.

- Someone who helps the child become familiar with the provision.

- Someone who meets children's individual needs and care needs (e.g. dressing, toileting, etc.).

- Someone who responds sensitively to children's feelings, ideas and behaviour.

- The person who acts as a point of contact with parents.

For children up to the age of two, this relationship is of crucial importance. Each baby has very individualised ways of feeding, sleeping and very different needs in terms of reassurance and comforting. The key person will begin by learning about the baby's routines and needs from the parent, gradually taking over during the settling-in period. The experiences of adult patients in hospitals tell us that being fed, washed and having your intimate care needs met by many different people is very stressful; the same is true for young children in nursery. The arrangement of the key person approach will include ensuring that, wherever possible, nappy-changing, feeding, settling to sleep and comforting will be undertaken by the key person, and babies will not simply be handed from one person to the next like a bag of potatoes. In many settings, a 'co-person' approach ensures that there is a second person who is also very familiar with caring for the baby, which reduces the impact of lunch breaks, shift patterns and all of the other reasons why a key person will not be available all the time.

These principles remain important throughout the early years phase, although differences in development and temperament mean that some children need consistent and individualised care throughout the early years, whereas others are more able to accept care and support from a range of people as they move through the end of the nursery phase and into reception.

Table 7.1 gives an example of a monitoring observation in a Baby Room with a focus on the key person approach.

Table 7.1

Names: Of teacher/room leader and staff undertaking observation.	Chantelle observing start of day in the Baby Room (Rehema, Sharon and Justine, apprentice).
Context: Date, time, place and children involved.	7.30-7.40.a.m. Arrival of two babies (Letitia and Dean) and transition from parent to key person.
Principles and values observed in action: • Equality. • Inclusion. • Respect for the Child.	Respect for the Child: the team work hard to tune into babies' communication and to give babies time to respond.
Characteristics of Effective Learning observed: • Playing and Exploring. • Active Learning. • Creating and Thinking Critically. Comment on Emotional Warmth and Quality of Care. Comment on children's Spiritual, Moral, Social and Cultural Development.	Playing and Exploring: the carpet area was set up with beautiful, natural materials for babies to touch, hold, smell, taste and explore. Active Learning: the team see babies as actively learning about the properties of objects. Emotional Warmth and Quality of Care: the room was very welcoming and calm for parents coming in. The team encourage parents to take their time, even though work/commuting schedules are tight. Every baby is individually greeted by the key person, in an individual way.

	Letitia was carried in by her mum and she indicated with her body that she did not want to be put down. Key person encouraged mum not to rush Letitia and very gently sang a song which encouraged Letitia to turn towards her. KP held out arms but Letitia snuggled back into her mother. KP asked apprentice to support the two other babies so she could focus just on Letitia. Encouraged mum to sit on sofa and all three shared a book which she read. Letitia laughed during book. KP said to mum, 'Best thing we can do is be clear now, say a gentle goodbye and pass her safely over to me on the sofa.' Letitia cried but was safe as her mum left. Letitia looked to KP for comfort and KP sat there for the next 15 minutes, first quietly comforting, then singing gently, and finally returning to the book. Letitia sad and KP gently sympathetic, not trying to distract or be jolly. After a few more minutes Letitia wriggled and indicated her desire to get down to the floor, KP gently put her by the carpet and stayed physically close to her, giving her time to look around and decide where to play.
Evidence of children making progress in their learning: • Concepts. • Attitudes. • Skills.	Progress observed: Letitia was especially drawn to the lemon yesterday in her Treasure Basket, so the team included a lemon amongst the resources on the carpet. Letitia soon found the lemon and spent time smelling it and holding it, turning it around slowly. Repeated opportunities to explore like this give Letitia a chance to express a choice and to deepen her experience of smelling and touching the lemon.
Evidence of how well teaching supports the learning of children at different ages, levels of development, and with special educational needs.	The range of materials on the floor enabled every child to get involved in exploration – shakeable items (the varnished maracas) were especially alluring to Dean, who is just starting to pick things up and grasp them. Jamal explored the feel of the pastry brush against his face and nose and laughed loudly at times. To do this, he had to co-ordinate hand/eye movements very carefully.

(Continued)

Table 7.1 (Continued)

Summary: What is enabling a good experience of care and good opportunities for learning?	• Calm, beautifully arranged room. • Exceptionally sensitive key person care enabled children to feel safe and secure at a sensitive time (transition from parent to key person). • Babies' interests noted, and provided for (e.g. the lemon) enabling them to develop their exploration.
Summary: What is holding children back?	• Although the music was soothing, perhaps it interfered with babies being able to hear language?

Post-observation dialogue:

The team have been reflecting on how to improve transition from parent to key person, when a child finds this hard. Last week Letitia had screamed as her mother tried to hand her to her KP and because both were standing up, the KP had been worried that Letitia might have fallen between their arms. Today – looks like the approach is better – safer and emotionally more supportive. Chantelle suggested that maybe they should offer to phone Letitia's mother later in the morning to reassure her everything was alright – once Letitia is settled, Justine could play with her to enable this? The team are putting more of an emphasis on the arrangement of the room and choice of materials to play with, as babies arrive one member of staff will keep doing this unless their key child arrives. Chantelle reflected that this looks to be working well. The team explained that the music was especially for Letitia, her mum had suggested it and they turn it off later in the morning as it can make it difficult to tune into the sounds babies make, and for the babies to tune into spoken language.

Outcomes/next steps (maximum of three):

Consider how parents might have further reassurance if their children find the start of day difficult.

Promoting positive behaviour

In the EYFS, promoting positive behaviour is very much bound up in the Prime Area of Personal, Social and Emotional Development. Whilst there are very high expectations of how children should behave and respond to adults in Ofsted's framework, there is also a recognition that in the EYFS children are just starting to learn about how to manage their feelings and behaviour in a group context. It is to be expected that young children will get angry, have tantrums, struggle to share, and say 'no' to adults. What is important is how adults respond, how they remain calm and positive, how they help children to learn and develop through these typical stages, and how they maintain an organised and purposeful learning environment. If adults react in angry, loud and stressed ways to children's challenges, behaviour can deteriorate even further.

Challenging behaviour can often be rethought as an opportunity for learning. Young children need adults to help them to learn about acceptable ways to manage themselves in a group setting. This helps children to 'self-regulate' – in other words, instead of merely following the rules and doing what they are told, they are aware of and manage their emotions and feelings, and they understand that this makes their nursery or class a happier and fairer place to be. Over time, this means that adults do not need to spend so much time enforcing rules, because the children understand why the rules are there and choose to follow them. This is sometimes called 'self-regulation', and the evidence suggests that helping children to develop their self-regulation is one of the most important things we can do in the early years. The *Sustained Shared Thinking and Emotional Well-Being (SSTEW) Scale for 2–5-Year-Olds Provision* (Siraj et al., 2015) is an excellent way to evaluate how well you promote children's wellbeing and help them to develop their self-regulation.

Staying safe online

It may seem that the section in the Ofsted framework about online safety is relevant only to older children, but this is definitely something that needs consideration. The main way to help young children stay safe online is through parent education, because their main way of getting online will be through using their parents' phones and, increasingly, iPads and tablets which have been bought for them.

Parents need to know how to use the settings in these devices to keep children safe from violence, pornography and other harmful material online. They also need to make sure that their children are confident to tell them if they do, despite those steps being taken, stumble across something that upsets or frighten them. If children fear being 'told off', they may say nothing. Practical workshops for parents, together with written guidance, can be very helpful. The NSPCC also offer a helpline to talk parents through how to set up parental controls and answer specific questions – search online for 'NSPCC online safety' to find out more.

Spiritual, Moral, Social and Cultural Development

Although there is now a Common Inspection Framework, it is only schools which are required by law to promote children's Spiritual, Moral, Social and Cultural Development (usually abbreviated to SMSC). There is a significant overlap between this duty and the duty to promote fundamental British values. There is non-statutory guidance from the Department for Education to advise school leaders and practitioners about this, available here: www.gov.uk/government/uploads/system/uploads/attachment_data/file/380595/SMSC_Guidance_Maintained_Schools.pdf.

Table 7.2 can be used to help you to show how you can ensure that children's SMSC runs through the framework of the EYFS like 'Brighton' through a stick of rock candy.

Table 7.2

Ofsted will look for the following features in children's spiritual development	Links to the EYFS
Ability to be reflective about their own beliefs, religious or otherwise, that inform their perspective on life and their interest in and respect for different people's faiths, feelings and values.	Understanding the World: People and Communities.
Sense of enjoyment and fascination in learning about themselves, others and the world around them.	Characteristics of Effective Learning: Active Learning.
Use of imagination and creativity in their learning.	Expressive Arts and Design: Being Imaginative.
Willingness to reflect on their experiences.	Characteristics of Effective Learning: Creating and Thinking Critically.
Ofsted will look for the following features in children's moral development	
Ability to recognise the difference between right and wrong and to readily apply this understanding in their own lives, recognise legal boundaries and, in so doing, respect the civil and criminal law of England.	Personal, Social and Emotional Development: Managing Feelings and Behaviour.
Understanding of the consequences of their behaviour and actions.	Personal, Social and Emotional Development: Managing Feelings and Behaviour.
Interest in investigating and offering reasoned views about moral and ethical issues and ability to understand and appreciate the viewpoints of others on these issues.	Personal, Social and Emotional Development: Managing Feelings and Behaviour. Understanding the World: People and Communities.
Ofsted will look for the following features in children's social development	
Use of a range of social skills in different contexts, for example working and socialising with other pupils, including those from different religious, ethnic and socio-economic backgrounds.	Personal, Social and Emotional Development: Managing Feelings and Behaviour. Understanding the World: People and Communities.
Willingness to participate in a variety of communities and social settings, including by volunteering, co-operating well with others and being able to resolve conflicts effectively.	Personal, Social and Emotional Development: Making Relationships.

Ofsted will look for the following features in children's social development	
Acceptance and engagement with the fundamental British values of democracy, the rule of law, individual liberty and mutual respect and tolerance of those with different faiths and beliefs; they develop and demonstrate skills and attitudes that will allow them to participate fully in and contribute positively to life in modern Britain.	Understanding the World: People and Communities.
Ofsted will look for the following features in children's cultural development	
Understanding and appreciation of the wide range of cultural influences that have shaped their own heritage and those of others.	Expressive Arts and Design: Exploring and Using Media and Materials.
Understanding and appreciation of the range of different cultures within school and further afield as an essential element of their preparation for life in modern Britain.	Understanding the World: People and Communities.
Knowledge of Britain's democratic parliamentary system and its central role in shaping our history and values, and in continuing to develop Britain.	*This type of knowledge would be too abstract for the large majority of children in the EYFS but it is underpinned by early experiences in:* Understanding the World: People and Communities. Personal, Social and Emotional Development: Managing Feelings and Behaviour.
Willingness to participate in and respond positively to artistic, musical, sporting and cultural opportunities.	Expressive Arts and Design: Exploring and Using Media and Materials. Physical Development: Moving and Handling.
Interest in exploring, improving understanding of and showing respect for different faiths and cultural diversity and the extent to which they understand, accept, respect and celebrate diversity, as shown by their tolerance and attitudes towards different religious, ethnic and socio-economic groups in the local, national and global communities.	Understanding the World: People and Communities.

Bullying

Combatting bullying is clearly important, but again this area is perhaps a little more complex in the EYFS than it is for older children. Interestingly, Ofsted's (2015e) *Early Years Inspection Handbook* makes just a single reference to 'bullying', and the EYFS Statutory Framework none at all. On the other hand, there are repeated references to 'bullying' in the *School Inspection Handbook* (Ofsted, 2015d).

It is also important to note that all schools (including maintained nursery schools) are required by law to have a behaviour policy in place which includes measures to prevent all forms of bullying among children. All schools are also required to log and analyse incidents of bullying, discriminatory and prejudicial behaviour, including racist, disability and homophobic bullying, use of derogatory language and racist incidents.

The Department for Education says that bullying is usually defined as behaviour which is:

- Repeated.

- Intended to hurt someone either physically or emotionally.

- Often aimed at certain groups, e.g. because of race, religion, gender or sexual orientation.

This type of bullying implies a degree of planning and intentionality which is unusual – though not impossible to see – in the early years. Many young children will find it difficult to manage to share, to involve others, or properly understand that their behaviour harms or hurts others. The young child who lashes out in a sudden fit of anger, or pushes another child away from the train track, or says 'you're not coming to my party' to upset another child, is unlikely to be a 'bully'.

At one time, it was thought that children up to the age of five were too young or too innocent to discriminate against others on the grounds of race, religion or identity. However, research suggests that even very young children are highly attuned to differences, and capable of showing hostile or fearful responses to others as a result. Young children will also echo the views of older children and adults around them, and some of those views may be discriminatory. In order for children to learn positively about diversity, and possibly to 'unlearn' discrimination, early years settings and practitioners need to be sensitive to times when children say things or use body language to exclude others or to express dislike. Children need time to think and talk about this – and will not be helped if they are simply told off, or if practitioners look the other way because it feels too difficult and controversial to do or say anything. There are several excellent books which explore these issues thoroughly and in a practical way (Lane, 2008; Siraj-Blatchford, 1994; Brown, 1998).

Reflection point

These questions may help you to consider the effectiveness of the steps that you are taking to improve the quality of teaching, learning and assessment:

- Do you use appropriate tools for self-evaluation, so you know where to focus your CPD and leadership in order to improve teaching?

- Do you balance your role in monitoring quality, with your role in improving practice through modelling, coaching and curriculum development? Lots of management and monitoring will not, in itself, make anything better.

- Does all your monitoring result in professional dialogue, with a focus on children's learning and care? Do you follow up action points regularly, and give staff the support and training they need to achieve them?

- Do you bring in others to observe with you (e.g. other experienced leaders, specialist consultants, practitioners who are also trained Ofsted inspectors) in order to help you sharpen your observation skills and challenge your thinking?

Thinking about the broad phases of development outlined in Part 1:

Table 7.3

Phase one: Practice which works for you.	You will need to consolidate this phase so that your teaching, learning and assessment will be Good. At earlier stages, you will probably Require Improvement. Your focus will be on making sure that everyone in the team is consistent in the 'basics' (e.g. in a nursery class, supporting children's Personal, Social and Emotional Development, Physical Development and early Communication, and encouraging their playing, exploring and active learning). You will keep new innovations and developments to a minimum until you are achieving this consistently.
Phase two: Practice which works for you, and is consistent with the research and evidence base.	Your teaching, learning and assessment will be consistently Good. You will be introducing tools like the SSTEW scale to apply research findings in order to develop some areas of highly effective practice.
Phase three: Developing leading-edge practice.	You will be considering research like the EPPSE project findings and using tools like the SSTEW scale regularly. You will be adapting these tools and research findings in the light of the very specific characteristics of your children and local context. Your teaching, learning and assessment will most likely be Outstanding.

8

The Common Inspection Framework

Outcomes

Introduction

The specific focus on 'outcomes' is, I would argue, the single most uncomfortable aspect of the Common Inspection Framework for early years practitioners. For anyone in a standalone early years setting, like a private nursery or a nursery school, it means thinking about children's 'outcomes' before they have even begun their compulsory education. At its worst, this can lead to an emphasis on where we want children to get to – their outcomes – rather than focussing on what is important for a young child *today*.

In her newsletter about the new framework, Gill Jones, Ofsted's Deputy Director of Early Education, usefully puts 'outcomes' into a more early-years-friendly context: 'we've ensured that the framework fully reflects provision for babies and toddlers, and the new "outcomes" judgement will focus heavily on the progress children make, given their starting points' (Ofsted, 2015a). That focus on *progress* is important, given the variability of children's development, and considering how summer-born children may be a full 11 months younger than their oldest classmates.

However, to avoid being over-critical of this focus on 'outcomes', it is worth recalling just how unequal children's life chances are in England. By the end of the EYFS, in the summer term of the reception year, a huge gap has opened up between children from low-income backgrounds and the rest.

⭐

As Ofsted state: 'the 19 percentage point gap between disadvantaged children and their better-off counterparts has remained unacceptably wide for too long'. I would argue that anyone who thinks fairness is important needs to pay attention to this.

At the time of writing, the Department for Education's (2016) *Reception Baseline Comparability Study* has concluded that the three different baseline assessment systems for reception are 'not sufficiently comparable to create a fair starting point from which to measure pupils' progress. As a result, the results cannot be used as the baseline for progress measures.' So they are no longer statutory. As a result, the Department for Education has decided to retain the Early Years Foundation Stage Profile for another year, until summer 2017. It is likely that there will be further announcements about Early Years assessment to come.

Whilst the Department for Education considers what the statutory measure for assessment in the early years will be, the following questions may help you to check whether your systems are fit for purpose:

- Starting points: How will you gather information about children's development, wellbeing and interests from previous settings (if applicable) and from parents? What assessments can you make in your context so that you gain a rounded picture of each child's starting points?

- How frequently will you update your system to track each child's progress, without becoming over-burdened? Consider whether you might update information more often for vulnerable children (those with special educational needs, or those eligible for the Early Years Pupil Premium, for example).

- Does your system allow you regularly to compare the outcomes of different groups (e.g. boys and girls or specific ethnic cohorts in your provision), so that you can take quick action to address inequalities? Can you compare the progress of the children with the lowest levels of development against the progress of the rest, so you can check they are making faster progress and the gap is closing?

- Does your system allow you to compare progress in different areas of learning, so that you can take action if one aspect of your curriculum does not seem to be as effective as the rest?

There are three further points to bear in mind. Firstly, remember to focus on impact. If you have a good system, and if it is telling you that boys make better progress than girls, make sure you are doing something about that. Try some different approaches in your provision and see whether they have a positive impact. If they do not, try something different. Similarly, if you can see progress is strong in communication, but weak in number, then think about how you will strengthen the teaching of maths and build on what works well in other areas. Use the information you have in real time to make a difference to the children. This work is not primarily about 'tracking' or 'data': it is about checking on how effective your provision is, and taking action speedily when necessary.

Secondly, remember that progress matters more than attainment overall. If children are making very strong progress from their starting points, then you are doing a good job – even if their development is still at below expected levels when they leave you. Over time, children who enjoy their learning and make strong progress will catch up. No-one states whether they got a Good Level of Development by the end of the EYFS on their CV. If you focus too much on levels of attainment, you may make erroneous judgements about your provision. For example, a summer-born child in reception is likely to need the same provision as a child who has just turned four in a nursery. If you do not expect children to sit for 45 minutes in a phonics group in nursery when they turn four, why should you expect that in reception? The whole point of assessment is to make sure you provide the provision, teaching and care a child needs to develop their learning. The national communication charity I CAN has argued, on the basis of research, that decisions to stream young children into groups by ability and to focus on formal learning too early, rather than play, speaking and listening, have very negative consequences for summer-born children. They end up hugely over-represented in the numbers of children with delayed speech and language. And that is not, by anyone's standards, a good outcome.

Finally, some settings deliberately assess children at low levels on entry, so they can more easily demonstrate progress to Ofsted. This is a foolish approach to take for a number of reasons. Firstly, you need accurate assessments to inform your planning and provision: if they are artificially low, they will be useless, and they may even lead to practitioners having lower expectations than they should. Secondly, you could easily trip up during your inspection if you do this: your inspector is very likely to spend time observing children new to the provision, talking with them, and comparing their judgements with the ones on your records. If there is an indication that your assessment is inaccurate, then your outcomes will also be called into question, and you could find everything unravelling very quickly.

Evaluating and demonstrating children's outcomes

It is easy to fall into a trap here. Demonstrating outcomes is *not* about having huge amounts of data and pages of evidence. In fact, the longer you and your colleagues spend on the bureaucratic processes of recording assessment and other information, the less time you will have to think about the children's needs and their learning. If practitioners say that they have too many observations to assess them and use them for planning, then I would advise them to do fewer observations. Just as it is disconcerting to spend time in early years provision and see staff inordinately hidden behind tablets snapping photos and writing notes, instead of interacting with children, it is also worrying if staff spend hours on their own compiling profile books and folders and hardly any time in professional dialogue about children's learning. Bulging scrapbooks, Profile Books or Special Books full of Post-its, photos and comments may be lovely, but they will not in themselves make any difference to children. We are here to care for the children and to help them learn – we are not writing their biographies

Secondly, beware ICT-based systems which rely on lots of assessment data and which promise to help you provide evidence of outcomes for Ofsted. You may find a system that helps you, but take a long and careful look at how much work it will take to feed in all that data. Is that really the best use of everyone's time in your school or setting? At a recent conference, I was even told by a delegate that her app-based system would automatically plan the next steps of learning for the children. That's nonsense – planning for learning will always require the involvement of practitioners, parents and children (depending on their age and development).

Observing and evaluating outcomes minute by minute in the provision

I have argued throughout this book that the best processes you can use as a leader involve professional dialogue, collaboration and challenge. In this spirit, the observation of children's experiences should be thought of as a joint endeavour and not a mock-Ofsted. It should result in considered reflection and actions to improve provision for children. Leave Ofsted-style grading to Ofsted: focus instead on what is effective about the provision, teaching and care, and how you can develop that further. If there are aspects of the provision which are holding back children's learning, they need addressing. A simple 'grade' will not inform your leadership, or help your team to improve continuously. Of course, if a practitioner is inadequate you will need to address that urgently, as discussed in Part 1, mindful of the fact that the early years are a sensitive period of learning. Those two-year-olds will not be two again: so, we have to act quickly if provision is not good enough.

Before you spend time observing the practice in a room, you might talk to the room leader or teacher and think about how you will prepare for your joint observation. You will want to ensure that you spend time observing some of the children who warrant a special focus – those who are more vulnerable, and those who are in receipt of the Early Years Pupil Premium, for example. By looking at the range of children's development, you will be able to look closely at whether the provision is well-pitched for most of the children. In a baby room for children from birth to two, if most of the children are over 18 months and developing well, you will expect to see much of the provision looking like the descriptions in the 8–20-month band of *Development Matters* (Early Education, 2012) But you will also be very mindful of the needs of young babies in the room and be looking for specific baby-provision like Treasure Basket play and very careful management of care routines.

On the other hand, in a nursery class for three- and four-year-olds where many are judged to be at lower levels of development, you will be expecting to see lots of the hands-on experiences set out in the 16–26-month band – messy play, plenty of time and space for home corner play and dressing up. You will expect to see a strong focus on learning through self-care activities like spreading margarine on crackers, cutting bananas and pouring drinks, and children being given plenty of help to learn to put on their own coats and other items of clothing.

After considering whether the provision looks right for the children, including those who are vulnerable and those who are making the strongest progress, you will be specifically looking for teaching which is helping children to take the next steps in their learning. In other words, some of the most important information about 'outcomes' comes from what you see happening minute by minute in the provision.

This means you have to be very focussed when you are observing provision. Table 8.1 gives an example by a practitioner who is training to be a leader and who has been asked to take part in a joint observation of two-year-old provision. This is what he wrote in the relevant section of the Sheringham pro forma.

Table 8.1

Evidence of children making progress in their learning: • Concepts. • Attitudes. • Skills.	Children can get their coats when they want to go outside. Practitioners help pull them on or zip them up when needed. This means they are becoming independent in the setting and developing their confidence.

There are several problems with this. Firstly, there is not enough detail about children's learning, or their progress. The observer has described what he has seen in general terms, without giving much of a 'feel' for what was happening that morning. Provision is described, but there is not enough detail about its impact. Each child in the provision is an individual, but they are referred to as one, as 'children' all the time. The downside will be that the post-observation dialogue is likely to be too general, and therefore will not help the practitioners to reflect and to improve on their practice. The observation also tells us nothing about the outcomes for the children – so that will be another job which will need to be done.

Table 8.2 gives an improved redraft of the section, following a discussion between the trainee leader and his mentor.

Evaluating outcomes through planning and assessment information

This is the third main way of checking outcomes. Many settings keep 'Special Books' or 'Learning Journeys' for every child. Sometimes, similar systems are used in online systems, bringing together photographs, observations and other

Table 8.2

Evidence of children making progress in their learning: • Concepts. • Attitudes. • Skills.	Amy goes to her coat peg, takes her coat off, and brings it to Chantelle. Stands still. Chantelle gets to her level and waits. Amy: 'Help.' Chantelle: 'You want help with your coat?' Amy: 'Help coat.' Chantelle helps Amy to put one arm in: 'Can you do the other arm?' Amy pushes her hand mostly into the sleeve. Chantelle helps her by pulling the sleeve back the rest of the way. Chantelle: 'Let's do it up together. I'll start the zip off.' She helps Amy to hold the zipper and says, 'Can you pull it up?' Amy pulls it up until it is zipped up. Amy is making progress in her language – from single words, to using two words with encouragement. Concepts: demonstrating 'up'. Attitudes: Amy is learning to persevere with a difficulty. Skills: motor skills, pushing arm/hand into sleeve, grasping zipper, pulling up.

notes. All too often, there is too much emphasis on quantity and not enough on quality and analysis. Here are some key questions to help you evaluate the quality of your system:

- Is someone taking an overview, so that there are regular updates for each child, and more regular updates for the most vulnerable children? It is not uncommon to find that one key person maintains extensive records about their children, and another has not updated the system for a month or more. This might mean some children are missing out.

- Does the system clearly show progress? If children's speech is being regularly and accurately written down, you will expect to see how a baby's vocalisations and gestures develop over time into speaking one or two words and making some sounds or using gestures with special meanings. For older children, you may see a move from single words, to two- or three-word sentences; you will want to see children beginning to use tenses accurately, too. You might have a photo of a two-year-old being helped onto a small climbing frame, and several months later the same child scrambling over a fallen tree in the park. Drawings of people will begin to show features over time: arms, legs, eyes, etc. If you cannot clearly see progress (or barriers to progress, which are being addressed) then your system is not fit for purpose.

- Can you hear the child's voice and the parent's voice? If children are encouraged to look back over their learning, they will be developing their metacognition (awareness of how they learn), which will strongly support the Characteristics of Effective Learning. They will make links between ideas and experiences over time. Parent voices will tell you how well home and the early years provision complement each other, and show the extent of the partnership. You might also help parents track their children's progress over time, and think of ways to help them, by using the parent's guide to the EYFS *What to Expect, When* (available free online here: www. foundationyears.org.uk/2015/03/what-to-expect-when-a-parents-guide).

- Where a child has additional needs, you will want the small but significant steps of progress to be made clear. If other professionals are involved, their assessments should inform yours.

You might also want to check for the following signs which indicate serious shortcomings:

- The system is erratically used: Some staff work to a high standard, but others are more haphazard, or books are poorly presented and spelled. These inconsistencies will mean that some children and families are getting much better support than others: that is not fair.

- There are lots of photos, like a scrapbook, but little evidence of detailed thinking about children's learning and progress. Pages of lovely photos of the children's Eid party will not tell you anything useful (but photos annotated with a child's conversation will tell you a lot about their language, and possibly their understanding of different cultures and religions).

- There are many generalised observations and photos: 'The children enjoyed visiting the farm, seeing the animals, and feeding the baby lambs.' This tells you nothing about the individual child, their learning, or their progress.

You will also want to consider planning documentation. The threads which show progress should be visible, running through short- and medium-term planning. For example, if you are looking at weekly planning you might see an evaluation stating that two children – Jason and Fatima – are making strong progress in their fine motor skills, and also making choices about items to stick down when designing their own collages. So, the next week's planning might include 'add smaller items to collage trolley (Jason and Fatima)'. Flicking on a month or two, you might find an adult-led activity for a small group of children, including Jason and Fatima, to take apart an old radio using screwdrivers aimed at developing their fine motor skills, strength and grip, and encouraging discussion about how things work. This will clearly show children making progress, and contribute to your view that outcomes are very positive. You are reading a kind of 'story' about the children's time in the provision. On the other hand, if the planning sheets show a series of different activities and resources being set out on different days without this sort of information, then you will not be seeing positive outcomes, and you are likely to be concerned that assessment is not being used formatively to develop the planning.

Reflection point

These questions may help you to consider the effectiveness of the steps you are taking to improve outcomes:

- Do you have a clear view of the progress of each child, in relation to their individual starting point? Can you compare the progress of different groups? Is the 'gap' closing between children who started at lower levels of development, and the rest? Do you have a clear view of the progress of children eligible for additional funding, children with special educational needs, and children learning English as an additional language? Are children with the highest levels of development sustaining their progress?

- Are you using the information in 'real time'? If your assessment information shows you that one group of children is making slower progress than another, do you use that information to revise your provision and check whether your changes are making a positive difference?

Thinking about the broad phases of development outlined in Part 1:

Table 8.3

Phase one: Practice which works for you.	You will need to consolidate this phase so that your outcomes will be Good. At earlier stages, you will probably Require Improvement. Your focus will be on making sure that practice is consistent: assessments are completed when children start, involving their parents, and you check that these are accurate. The progress of individuals, and of groups of children, is carefully monitored and action is taken promptly where needed. Assessment is used formatively in planning documents, and you can see the progress children are making. Observations and assessments of children are proportionate – just what you need to inform planning and to track progress, and no more. You gain a consistent picture of progress from observing the provision, from children's profiles, and from the planning and assessment information.
Phase two: Practice which works for you, and is consistent with the research and evidence base.	Children are making strong and sustained progress from their different starting points, and you are putting a particular emphasis on areas which will boost progress across the whole of the EYFS. For example, you are focusing on the characteristics of effective learning, or developing children's self-regulation.
Phase three: Developing leading-edge practice.	You are applying research and best practice in specific areas in order to boost outcomes for the most vulnerable. For example, you might be using the Early Years Toolkit from the Education Endowment Foundation (https://educationendowmentfoundation.org.uk/evidence/early-years-toolkit) to find effective practice to narrow the gap between children eligible for the Early Years Pupil Premium and the rest.

Your outcomes will most likely be Outstanding. |

9

Bringing it all together

How effective is your early years provision?

One of the most difficult things we have to do as leaders is to bring information together to think about it, and then act on it. It is very common to feel like King Canute, stuck on the beach as the waves roll over us. Sometimes, I even wonder if we get tempted to be more and more busy in order to put off the difficult tasks of stopping, thinking and acting. Getting busy, tidying things up, sorting things out and generally bustling about can provide a kind of comfort. But thinking, exercising judgement, and then making changes is really hard work. It generally involves difficult conversations with people, or having to make a tough choice between two unpleasant options. Do I keep putting a lot of time into helping a member of my team become a better practitioner, even though there has not been much to show for my efforts over the last few months? Or do I start formal procedures around capability, which will be stressful, upsetting and unsettle the rest of the team too?

But, putting Ofsted to one side for a moment, we have to spend time synthesising the information we have and putting it to good effect. Ideally, you should create and protect time to do this regularly, and you should engage with others who can help develop and also challenge your thinking: your deputy, a governor or member of your advisory board, someone you know and trust from another setting, or an external consultant.

Throughout the book, I have argued that an extensive 'tick box' approach is not a good use of your time. Perhaps you have previously taken part in a quality assurance scheme that involved folders full of evidence being collated and assessed, run by a professional association or by your local authority?

Far too often, these schemes put a premium on bureaucracy with endless audit forms to fill in. Far more effective, in my opinion, are processes which are based on professional dialogue and making professional judgements. Keep trying to answer the question, 'What would it be like to be a child here?' and focus on what you notice that tells you that the children feel safe, cared for and encouraged to learn.

You will need to have a cycle of bringing together and analysing all the information you have. Table 9.1 gives an example, which is for a setting that is solidly Good, fully compliant with statutory requirements and working hard to improve.

Table 9.1

Every month	Review children's attendance, and offer extra support to families who are not managing to bring their child in regularly or on time. Ask for consent to refer families on for Children's Centre family support if they need more help than you can offer.
	Review the progress and wellbeing of children eligible for the Early Years Pupil Premium, and any other children who may be vulnerable. If the help you are giving is not making a difference, consider different approaches and keep checking up.
Every three months	Check the progress and wellbeing of every child in a manageable way (e.g. by meeting with the room leader and looking at each child in turn). Identify children who may need extra support, or who may need further assessment to identify special needs or other barriers to their learning. Keep checking regularly on each child causing concern by observing the child, speaking to the key person and speaking to the parents.
	Bring together any observations of practice which have been completed for performance management purposes or monitoring purposes. Check that there is good coverage of all areas of the EYFS, and identify any areas which need to be checked in the next three months.
	Look for any common themes and for strengths and weaknesses.
	What support, training or other activities will you need to do in order to promote further improvement?
	Work with all staff to review the impact of the improvement plan to date:
	• What is going well – where do we have evidence that we are making the improvements which we planned? • What is not going so well – where do we need to intensify our efforts? • What new challenges have emerged which we need to work on together?

(Continued)

Table 9.1 (Continued)

Every six months	Thoroughly check compliance with all aspects of the EYFS Statutory Framework and with safeguarding requirements.
	Carry out a short survey of parents for their views in a specific area (e.g. how well informed they are about their child's wellbeing and progress; how well the settling in process worked for them and their child).
	Take a Learning Walk with a governor/member of the management board with a specific focus (e.g. how well does the outdoors promote children's health, wellbeing and learning?).
Every year	Arrange for a 'review day' with a colleague from another setting and a local authority adviser to check on the accuracy of self-evaluation and the impact of the improvement plan.
	Ask key partners to help you review the impact of the provision through half hour face-to-face meetings or phone calls – here are two examples:
	Specialist agencies (e.g. Speech and Language Therapist):
	• How well have we worked together with you? • Thinking of specific children: How good has their progress been from their starting points? Have we succeeded in giving them the extra help you recommended? • What should we do better next year?
	Schools or settings which children transfer to:
	• How well have we worked together with you? • Thinking of specific children: How well did the arrangements we made help them make a smooth transition? • How useful did you find the information we shared with you about children's care needs and their learning? • What should we do better next year?

Here is what we do with the partner schools and settings within our Teaching School Alliance at Sheringham on the 'review day' – you will, of course, need to adapt this to suit your own needs.

We arrange a day with a leader from another setting or with an external consultant in order to review every aspect of the provision. This creates a team of at least two 'improvement partners' working together, at least one from the setting and at least one from outside the setting.

The week before, the setting shares two key documents: its current self-evaluation document, and its current improvement plan.

On the day, the partners spend the majority of the time engaged in joint observations of practice, together with talking to parents and talking to governors. This information is then discussed with reference to our self-evaluation document and our current improvement plan. We consider whether our self-evaluation is accurate, and where it might need to be changed. We look at whether there is evidence that our improvement plan is having a positive effect. We compare our observations of practice against our outcomes for children: if practice looks strong in supporting children's Understanding of the World, is that reflected in strong outcomes? Where outcomes are weaker, is practice weaker and are we doing enough to improve?

We spend the last hour and a half of the day going through all the information we have to summarise which practice we have noticed is effective, and where we need to do more to improve. Where we need to make improvements, we keep the action points down to one or two items, and we make sure that we know exactly who will be doing what, and what the timescales will be.

Conclusions

In this second part of the book, I have argued that leaders and managers in all kinds of early years provision need to begin with a strong vision, and with ambitions for the children, their families and the staff team. This vision and ambition is, in my view, best articulated in a straightforward way: How are we going to make this setting a great place where a child can enjoy, learn and develop, and be prepared for the next phases of life and learning?

Effective settings are carefully and rigorously managed: they take actions and make improvements through carefully planned steps, supporting staff with continuous professional development and time to reflect. Everything is carefully monitored and considered in terms of the outcomes for the children. The focus is not on being busy, but on doing the right things that will make a positive difference.

You will determine the effectiveness of your leadership and management: firstly by considering your impact in terms of vision, ambition, and how well your cycle of improvement and self-evaluation works. You will also need always to be compliant with the EYFS Statutory Framework, all relevant safeguarding legislation, and other statutory requirements. Secondly, you will consider the other three areas of the Ofsted framework: teaching, learning and assessment; personal development, behaviour and welfare; and outcomes for children. For Ofsted, everything is about impact: you might have a great vision, high ambition, and good systems, but your leadership and management is only as good as your impact in those three areas. For that reason, although leadership and management comes first in the Common Inspection Framework, you need to self-evaluate it last: it rests on the other three.

You will need to have a cycle of evaluating the quality of your provision which you can realistically stick to, and which involves regular professional dialogue and consideration of children's experiences. You need to spend time thinking about what your evaluations tell you about the quality of your provision, and what you should be doing to make sure that you keep improving. You need to make time so that you can think, talk with others, and make the most accurate judgements possible. That will help you to be a careful and considered leader who can skilfully guide the team and focus on the areas which need the most attention. It will also mean that you are well prepared for the day that Ofsted calls, and for the period after your inspection, which are the themes of the next part of the book.

PART 3

YOUR INSPECTION DAY AND BEYOND

Introduction

In the previous parts of this book, I argued that early years settings need to have systems and structures in place to support the continuing professional development of their teams. We need to be able to make accurate self-evaluations which will in turn inform our plans and bring about improvements to our provision. All of those aspects require ambitious leadership, combined with the mentoring and coaching which will support your team in reflecting on and developing their practice.

Preparing for your Ofsted inspection also means knowing about the impact of all your work, and coming back to a central question to focus your reflections: 'What is it like to be a child here?' Leaders also need to be prepared, by understanding the Ofsted inspection framework, and having the essential information ready at hand. The worst type of inspection experience happens when staff are rushing around and reacting to the demands of their inspector. Of course, your inspection will be demanding and rigorous, and that means you may find it stressful. But, for the majority of the time, you should feel like you are working collaboratively with someone who brings the experience and training to make judgements about quality which are grounded in evidence. In that sense, inspections are an opportunity for our professional development and learning, as well as fulfilling the important role of public accountability: are we spending public money well, and are we making sure that we do our very best for young children at this important time in their lives?

10

Inspection day

Being confident and ready for your inspection

You will generally have some notification before Ofsted actually arrive. If you are in a pre-school, nursery or a school-based EYFS provision you will be contacted half a day before your inspection. Sessional provisions, like crèches, will have up to a day's notice and childminders will have about a week's notice. However, Ofsted will not give any notice to Inadequate provisions, or where they are conducting a priority inspection because there is a well-grounded concern.

In practice, what this means is that you should always be ready for inspection – after all, there will not be much you can prepare in just half a day. You should have key documents readily at hand, and be familiar with them all.

The following information will also be appreciated by your inspector:

- A list of your whole staff team, showing names, roles, and which team or class each individual is in.

- The names of your different rooms or classes.

- Routines of the day: what time you open and close, when children have lunch, and any other regular times (e.g. what time afternoon children come in; when you offer particular sessions like music, or Forest School).

- A breakdown of the children on roll, showing the pattern of attendance (for example, how many full-time, how many part-time), ages, numbers of boys and girls, main ethnicities, and how many children are eligible for the Early Years Pupil Premium.

- The current rate of attendance and absence (for example, in the last year, the last month, and on the day of inspection).

Arrival

When your inspector arrives, make sure that you check their official Ofsted identification badge and then sign them in like any other visitor. Inspectors will not routinely carry an enhanced DBS certificate. If you have any concerns or doubts about identity, then phone Ofsted's National Business Unit on 0300 123 4234. The inspector will briefly talk to you about how the inspection will be carried out, but, because time is so short, she or he will be keen to start inspecting as soon as possible. If you are in a school, the inspector or inspectors will be introduced to the whole staff at the beginning of the day, and will come into the early years provision at a time of their choosing. They will expect you to keep working as normal.

It is always a good idea to be confident and courteous, and to remember that inspectors are human beings too! They will appreciate a cup of tea or coffee, a confidential room or area to use, and being shown where the toilets are.

A very positive way to start off the inspection is by showing the inspector round the provision. This gives you a chance to explain what is happening, why, and how it reflects your aims and your ethos. Point out features of your provision and explain how they help the children feel safe and secure, and make strong progress in their learning. Always try to talk about impact, just like you have in your self-evaluation: so, rather than saying, 'we have a lovely graphics area here, which we always keep well stocked', say something like:

> because we have a lovely graphics area here, children are motivated to try all the different resources. We change them regularly to keep children interested in coming back regularly. Our displays over here show just some of the ways that children make marks and start on the early stages of writing, and I can tell you some more about the progress they make later.

If your provision follows a particular approach, like Montessori, Steiner or HighScope, then make sure that your inspector has an understanding of this. Show specific examples of your approach in action and explain the rationale behind them, and how they help children to feel safe and secure, and to make strong progress. If you have permission from the Department for Education to disapply aspects of the EYFS in line with your approach, make sure your inspector knows this and understands the reasoning behind it.

Observing staff together

Your inspector will ask if you would like to undertake joint observations, and you should definitely seize this opportunity. Here are some useful things to bear in mind whilst you are observing:

- **What is helping the children to learn?** Note down when you see good care routines, a well-organised and planned environment and good deployment of staff. Always comment on the impact of what you are seeing, for example: 'Bobbi and Clem are at the snack table. They can help themselves to crackers and independently spread them with margarine, so they are developing their fine motor skills. Dee asks them if they would like milk or water to drink, Bobbi says, "Juice, please," and Clem says, "It's just milk or water, they don't have any sugar" – children are being helped to make healthy choices.'

- **How effectively are staff helping children to make progress in their learning?** Note down indications that staff know the different starting points and needs of the individual children. Listen out for times when children expand on what they are saying because of the encouragement of a member of staff, or become engaged in their play because of the help or guidance they receive.

- **Especially for babies and young toddlers:** Note down where the key person approach is helping children to develop strong relationships and develop their sense of self and security.

You will know the children much better than the inspector, so you will be able to draw the inspector's attention to a moment which is particularly significant for an individual child. Where possible, talk about what has happened before: point out the child who has needed many weeks of support to be able to come in calmly, or the child who would only play in one or two areas but is now confidently accessing the whole room.

You will also know if something is not typical: perhaps a practitioner is having a bad day, or a child is not responding to things in their usual way. Think quickly on your feet – what can you offer your inspector to give a more accurate view of how things are over time. Do you have a recent example of when you observed the practitioner, when she or he was working effectively? Can you provide evidence that a child normally enjoys their time in nursery through their Special Book? Everyone can have a bad day: what Ofsted are trying to find out is the typical quality and effectiveness of your provision.

If there is a member of the team who is less effective than the others, then be open about this: tell your inspector why you think that, and the steps you are taking to address the situation. If the practitioner's practice is improving, then give examples. If it is not, explain what you are doing through your capability or disciplinary processes. Tell your inspector how you are minimising the impact on the children. For example, perhaps another member of staff is providing support at key group time to ensure consistent quality, or you are checking Special Books weekly and making changes where necessary. No team is perfect: what matters is that you can show how you act appropriately, decisively and firmly in the interests of the children.

It is very important that you can demonstrate that your judgement is sound. So, if you talk over the observation with the inspector, or if you offer feedback to the practitioner in front of the inspector, make sure that what you say is sound and is informed by what you saw. It is not advisable to try to give a positive spin – feed back accurately what you saw and what you thought. Otherwise, your inspector may come to the conclusion that you do not have the necessary skills to judge how effective your provision is. That will call the accuracy of your self-evaluation into question, which in turn will make your inspection a more difficult experience.

Ideally, your judgements about how effective the provision is will largely coincide with your inspector's. Ofsted plan for inspections to be done *with* you, and not done *to* you. Your early years expertise and your knowledge of the staff, children and families should help your inspector to gain a rounded view of your provision. This, in turn, will mean that your inspection will serve as a combination of a validation of your work, and an opportunity for professional dialogue and challenge.

However, the process of inspection is never going to be perfect, so there are likely to be at least some points where you and your inspector take a different view. In these cases, you need to be able to put across your view in a way which is professional, calm and appropriately assertive. Go back to the evidence that you have recorded and ask your inspector what they saw. Explain why you have come to your conclusion about the effectiveness of what you saw, if your inspector is taking a more negative view. Draw on previous observations to show typical quality over time, and link those observations to outcomes. Share any previously completed joint observations with professionals from outside your team – for example, advisory staff from the local authority, or experienced and specialist early years consultants.

During the inspection, generally towards the end, the inspector will talk to you about any Outstanding or Inadequate practice that has been seen. If there are serious concerns which might lead to an Inadequate judgement, you will be alerted to these. You will also have an opportunity to raise any concerns you might have about the conduct of the inspection or the inspector. You will be given an opportunity to find out about how the evidence collected will inform the judgements at the end. These areas of discussion are all highly important, so make sure you are calm, collected and in a suitable place. Keep brief notes, and tell your inspector if there is anything you do not do not agree with, or do not understand

If necessary, you could make a formal complaint, and this is discussed below. But it is much better to raise any issues, concerns or points for clarification *during* your inspection. Try to resolve them there and then. You will often find that there has simply been a misunderstanding, or that some further discussion makes things clearer.

Receiving feedback and responding to your report

Once your inspector has enough evidence, he or she will need some time to review all the information and to finalise judgements. This will give you some time to speak to your team, check that they are feeling okay, and offer some reassurance if needed.

Generally, your feedback should not present you with any surprises. If you have maintained dialogue with your inspector throughout the process, you should already have a good idea of what the key judgements will be. You should always have at least one other person with you for feedback: for example, the chair of your management board, your chair of governors, or another similarly senior person. You may wish to have your deputy. Ask the person with you to keep a record of the key points from the feedback. If there is anything which you do not understand, ask the inspector to explain it to you.

So, if you are told that 'staff do not always encourage children to share their experiences and observations, to develop their communication skills further', then ask your inspector for examples of what they mean. You can use those examples to help yourself and your team to reflect on your practice and think about how you might improve.

Where your inspector recommends action points for improvement, you will be invited to comment on the draft wording. This means you can help to phrase them so they are accurate and helpful, although the final choice of wording remains with Ofsted.

Finally, your inspector will make it clear that the outcomes of your inspection are confidential until the report is published. The only exception to this is if your provision is going to be judged Inadequate, in which case you must tell your local authority.

Disagreements and challenges

The large majority of inspections proceed smoothly, and generally practitioners say that they are happy with the conduct of the inspection and its outcomes. However, if there is something which you disagree with, then it is important to state that clearly during the feedback meeting. You should say clearly what your disagreement is, and explain it.

For example, imagine that you were told that 'staff are not always encouraging children to talk about and share their experiences', and you do not think that this is accurate. Firstly, ask for clarification: can the inspector provide examples, and explain why that judgement was made? If your inspector can bring forward examples of what was observed, with perhaps another source of evidence (children's assessment records, or conversations with parents) then you have probably learnt something new and important about your provision, even if you do not feel very happy about it. But if you feel the inspector does not have adequate evidence, you could challenge with a comment like:

> I don't agree with this judgement. Our own monitoring of the provision shows that staff consistently ask children to share and talk about their experiences, so what you saw on that occasion was not typical. Our assessment information also shows that children are making strong progress in their communication, so we would argue that the provision is effective over time.

As a general rule, challenges and complaints will only succeed in changing Ofsted's judgements if they are supported by evidence which was available to the inspector at the time of the inspection. You should raise any issues, concerns or inaccuracies as soon as possible: anything that is raised for the first time after the inspection is very unlikely to be supported. It cannot be stated too strongly that you should be listening to your staff throughout the inspection so that you can raise any concerns immediately.

You can find more information about making complaints by searching online for 'Ofsted Complaints Procedure'. You must make a complaint within ten working days of the incident.

Managing the publication of your inspection report

Your final Ofsted report is an important document. It may be the first thing that a parent reads about your provision before deciding whether to apply for a place. It will affect your staff team, potentially providing a boost to their professional pride – or fuel for their disappointment.

As soon as the report is published, spend time talking with your staff about it. Give them a chance to ask any questions they might have. People will often narrow their focus to the aspects which they see as negative, so help to make sure team members keep a balanced view and celebrate the positive findings. Staff are likely to feel much better about areas for improvement if they know that you will be working collaboratively with them on a plan to address them.

If you are judged Requires Improvement or Inadequate, then many or even all of your team are likely to feel upset, demoralised and angry. The way you handle this will make a big difference, for good or for ill. Whatever you think about the rights and wrongs of the judgement, you need to project confidence. After giving your team the opportunity to talk about their opinions and their feelings, it will be important to have a moment when you look forward together: there is a job to do to improve the setting, and you need everyone to work together and work hard. The least helpful reaction will be to nurse any feelings that you have been hard done by.

Parents will, of course, be very interested in the report, which you need to share with them on publication. If you have a Good or Outstanding judgement, a covering letter can highlight the key aspects you are most proud of. Parents will also want to know what you are planning to do in response to the action points, so outline what you will be doing, and tell them that you will be asking them periodically to help you review the impact. A Good or Outstanding report will also give you the chance to gain some further publicity: local papers are generally pleased to photograph staff with happy young children celebrating a successful Ofsted report, and local councillors, MPs and others may be happy to join in.

Settings which achieve an Outstanding judgement from Ofsted are expected to take part in activities to share their effective practice more widely, so that others can learn from it. Sharing and developing practice in collaboration with other settings is discussed in detail below.

If your report judges you to be less than Good, be open, confident and forward-looking when you communicate with parents. State your determination to make the necessary improvements. Offer to meet with any parent who wants to know more, or who is concerned. Tell parents how you will travel with them in the journey towards improving quality.

Using your Ofsted report to help you to improve further

As I have consistently argued in this book, Ofsted should not be your driver. You know your setting better than anyone, and you have multiple sources of information to tell you how good you are, and what you need to do to improve further. Ofsted have visited for one or two days and taken some snapshots: you have the whole film.

In keeping with this approach, the first thing to think about after your inspection is what you have learnt about the accuracy of your self-evaluation. Did you generally agree with your Ofsted inspector about the quality of provision? What did you learn from having a different and, perhaps, more practised and sharper professional alongside you?

The next area I would argue that you should focus on, is how good your plans to improve are. During your inspection, did you find that the actions you were taking in order to improve were showing good results and positive early impact? Or did you find that things were not as consistent as you thought, or that staff had not been able to implement training as well as you hoped?

You certainly need to think carefully about the action points you have been given, and how you will address them. The next time Ofsted come, one of the very first things they will look at will be your previous inspection. So make sure you start to address what they recommended straight away, and sustain that activity until the next inspection.

Once you have thought about these three areas, and built your ideas into your ongoing improvement plan, put Ofsted to the back of your mind. It is not helpful to obsess over the details of your inspection report. Keep up your work as a team to develop your practice, professionalism, levels of training and your qualifications. The surest way forward is to pull together:

- Your self-evaluation.
- The findings of challenging reviews and inspections.
- Continuous professional development.
- A range of information about the wellbeing and progress of the children.
- Your improvement plan.

That way, you are becoming a self-improving early years setting. You are paying attention to the signals and information you receive from outside your setting, and you are making yourself accountable to parents and others: but fundamentally your team is taking charge of its own destiny.

A self-improving early years system

As we approach the end of this book, now is perhaps a good time to take a quick look back over the recent history of inspecting and improving early years practice. Understanding the past can help us to think about and engage with the future.

Several decades ago, when I trained to be a teacher, there were few requirements for early years providers beyond basic legislation around ratios, hygiene and space. Expectations were sometimes low. In my first school, if a member of the nursery team was off sick, then the whole provision would be closed for the day. The headteacher judged that, as it was not statutory, it was not a good use of money when there were so many other demands on the staffing budget. That would be unthinkable now.

Back in the late 1980s, local social services inspectors checked day nurseries and childminders, and Her Majesty's Inspectorate oversaw early education in schools, reviewing the course of its expansion and sharing examples of good practice. There was no Ofsted, but local authorities had their own inspectors. In practice, there was a great deal of local variability. The focus was largely on compliance, not 'continuous improvement'.

All that changed for schools with the decision in 1990 to let schools hold and manage their own budgets and with the creation of Ofsted in 1992. Schools began to have development or improvement plans, linked to their budgets, with specially tailored training or consultancy. Increasingly, they determined their own direction, and Ofsted set the pace more than the local authority. This tendency has intensified in recent years, with the development of academies and free schools. The role of the local authority is in serious decline.

Whilst private, voluntary and community nurseries have always been independent and managed their own budgets, in other respects their journey has been similar to that of schools. Before Ofsted moved into regulating and inspecting childcare and early education in 2001, settings outside of schools were inspected by local authorities to check their compliance with the Daycare Standards.

At first, Ofsted's approach to the early years was heavily influenced by this compliance model. Sometimes, there seemed to be so much focus on correct documentation and policies that the experiences of the children hardly got a mention. Parallel to this change, however, local authorities massively expanded their early years advisory teams. Huge sums of money were spent on training and improving the levels of qualification and standards of practice. Although there were serious shortcomings in this approach, especially with the quality and consistency of qualifications, there is little doubt that the sector became more professionalised and more focussed on improving practice.

At a policy level, there is now a great deal of consistency across school and private, voluntary and independent settings. The statutory 2014 Early Years Foundation Stage provides a single set of requirements and a single curriculum overarching all early years providers. There are large numbers of graduate Early Years Professionals and Early Years Teachers working in all sectors. And, of course, Ofsted's Common Inspection Framework applies to everyone.

There are still, of course, important differences. Early Years Teachers do not command the salary or levels of ongoing professional support which are enjoyed by Qualified Teachers working in schools. The Common Inspection Framework is being implemented by two very different workforces. Funding levels vary hugely across the sectors, too. Schools draw down many more resources, as well as being required to meet different standards around special educational needs and higher minimum levels of staff qualification.

All the same, settings and practitioners in all sectors now have more in common than ever before: far more brings us together, than divides us. At the same time, the support available from local authorities is melting away like an ice cube in the sun. So, in this final part of the book, I am arguing that the way forward is for us to work together in our own, chosen groups and partnerships.

What is a self-improving early years system?

A system-approach to improvement in the early years involves practitioners working closely together. This entails a commitment to continuous professional development and an openness to innovation, with cycles of action and self-evaluation. It is about joint practice development: if a large group of practitioners can combine their efforts to focus on an area of practice, read the research, and develop new approaches together, that will be more powerful than a few people in small settings, in isolation from each other. As a leader and manager, I would struggle to find the time to read the research on the Education Endowment Foundation's website about self-regulation, and our setting would struggle to afford the costs of bringing in a consultant to work in a sustained way with us. But, if we combine with a group of other settings, then we can jointly pay for a consultant, who can help us navigate the research and develop new practice together.

Joint practice development means that you can focus on what matters in your specific context, with an emphasis on improving practice over time. You will not simply be falling in with what someone else thinks should be your priority. Nor will your team be attending a one-off training day which feels irrelevant to the day-to-day realities of your setting.

A successful example of how to start off joint practice development comes from the Born4Life Project, an international practitioner-led research initiative developed by International Early Years (www.ieytoday.co.uk) in collaboration with the Early Years Excellence Learning Alliance and other early years collaboratives. Within the alliance, settings work together using an approach which they call 'I wonder if'. After identifying an area for improvement, practitioners outline a statement to summarise what they are working together on. For example, if practitioners found that toddlers entering their provision were experiencing high levels of distress during the settling-in period, they might pose this question: 'I wonder what would happen if we offered home visits before children started?' The approach then asks practitioners to outline the planned benefits for key stakeholder groups, which might be as in Table 10.1.

The 'I wonder if' plan proceeds with a section outlining what the intervention will look like in practice, as in the box below.

Table 10.1

Children	Parents	Setting
By having a little familiarity with their key person on the first day of settling in, children might develop a special relationship and turn to their key person both for play and for comfort.	Parents would know one person amongst the 'sea of faces', so they would be more confident about their child's first days.	The setting will benefit from calmer and happier children in the longer run, and key people will find their roles more fulfilling if they have a special relationship with their key children and their parents.

Our settling-in observations from January show that toddlers found it difficult when they started and showed distress through upset and angry behaviour. Wellbeing came out at low levels, as measured by the Leuven scale. We are going to set up a pilot so the children starting in February will be home visited before they start. At the home visit the key person will mostly focus on playing with the child, and finding out some key information so that toys or activities can be prepared specially to suit the child's interests on their first day and beyond. We are going to use the Leuven scale and discussions with parents to judge the children's wellbeing and we will compare these findings with the information from January. We will use our professional judgement to make an overall assessment of this change, because we know children's development is very individual and differences in wellbeing may be down to that individuality rather than our practice.

The final section of the plan asks the practitioners to evaluate the impact of the new practice on the children's social, emotional and language development, and to identify any further impact for other children.

If you use 'I wonder if' within your team, this would be an example of how you are becoming a self-improving setting. If a group of practitioners innovate new practice across settings, training together, implementing the approach in a way which is tailored specifically to their setting, and then evaluating the outcomes both individually and collectively, then they are becoming a 'self-improving system' (Figure 10.1).

In some areas, all types of early years providers can engage with an existing self-improving system by joining their local Teaching School Alliance – you can find out more about Teaching Schools and where they are on the Teaching School Council's website at www.tscouncil.org.uk.

Alternatively, you might wish to form your own partnership with local early years settings, to focus on a key issue like continuing professional development, leadership development, or inclusion and special educational needs. David H. Hargreaves (2012), one of the leading thinkers who has developed the model of the self-improving system in England, makes a useful distinction between 'shallow partnerships' and 'deep partnerships'. Shallow partnerships are generally short-term or fixed-term relationships affecting just a few aspects

The EYELA Project

Our improvement issue is _____

_____

_____

Who is affected by the issue? _____

I wonder if we _____

_____

_____

What have you xxx to do the change and improve this xxx?

What would be better for ...?

Children	Parents	Setting

(What outcome are you looking for, by when and how will you know you have been successful?)

(Continued)

Figure 10.1 (Continued)

The EYELA Project

What will the intervention look like in practice?

(What are the actions you are going to try to improve/resolve the issue?)

(To be completed after actions have been implemented)

How has this impacted on children's social, emotional and language development?

-
-
-
-

How has this impacted on other children in the setting?

Figure 10.1 "I wonder if" planning format from the Early Years Excellence Learning Alliance (EYELA) and Born4Life

of each setting's work and a small number of people, whereas 'deep partnerships' are enduring and will generally affect everything and everyone in the organisations involved.

Reflection point

Your engagement with wider partnerships needs to be informed by careful consideration of your current development and needs as a setting. If constant day-to-day management is needed to make sure the provision is effective, then you will not want to spend time out of your setting engaging in discussions and building partnerships. The only reasons to engage in partnerships are to make sure the children have an appropriate experience of their early education, make the best possible progress, and are ready, willing and able to continue as successful learners.

Thinking about the three broad phases of your provision's development in relationship to partnerships:

Table 10.2

Phase one: Practice which works for you.	As you work to develop and consolidate the basics of effective practice, you will need the support and challenge of a 'second pair of eyes', like a local leader with a strong track record, or a recommended consultant. You will wish to draw on the expertise of a local partnership, like a Teaching School Alliance, but, at this stage, you may not feel ready to offer anything back – it may be a 'shallow partnership'.
Phase two: Practice which works for you, and is consistent with the research and evidence base.	At this stage, joint practice development is likely to be an appropriate way for you to improve your effectiveness. It is much easier to engage with research and evidence in a working group, than on your own. Partners can offer both support, and challenge, as you seek to do this. You are moving towards a 'deep partnership'.
Phase three: Developing leading-edge practice.	Once you are securely developing evidence-informed practice in your own setting, you will be getting ready to take on leadership and help other settings and colleagues. Your setting's highly effective practice will inspire and motivate colleagues. Their challenges and reflections with you will help you to improve even further. You are developing a 'deep partnership'.

Concluding thoughts

In 2013, Ofsted published a very useful short report about effective leadership in the early years, *Getting it Right First Time: Achieving and Maintaining High-Quality*

Early Years Provision. The report celebrates many of the characteristics of effective leadership in the early years which I have also tried to reflect throughout this book: a passion for the phase, in-depth specialist knowledge, a commitment to staff development and professionalism, and an openness to working with others and being challenged.

It is through determined action in these broad areas that the quality of early years provision will improve in England, and in particular that some of the most difficult remaining challenges can be overcome. Children in poorer communities are still more likely to attend low-quality early years provision than those who live in more affluent neighbourhoods. Although quality has improved considerably *in general* across the early years sector, there are still large numbers of settings and schools which seem to be stuck in a Requires Improvement rut.

That means that, on top of the qualities needed to bring about and sustain improving practice in our own settings, we also need to develop new qualities as leaders: a commitment to working together and caring about children in general, not just the children in our setting.

New inspection frameworks at Ofsted and new policies from government come and go, like showers in April. There are, however, deeper and longer seasons in professional practice. Philosophical approaches, like those drawing on Froebel, Montessori, Steiner and others, have shared their deeply held convictions about the uniqueness and special value of every child for decades, even centuries. Professional, practice-oriented approaches drawing on Reggio Emilia in northern Italy, Forest Schools in Denmark, maintained nursery schools in Britain or HighScope in the United States serve a similar function.

So, to return to the argument which I began to outline at the beginning of this book, we should be working to develop our teams and our practice because of our commitment as professionals. Ofsted is important, because it is through inspection that we are accountable to parents and other local people in the English system. But its importance is at the end of the cycle, to validate our work publicly. We are responsible for the whole cycle, from beginning to end, to make sure that we provide as well as we can for each and every child and their family.

In early 2016, Gill Jones, Ofsted's Deputy Director of Early Education, spoke to leaders from London's Early Years Teaching Schools and challenged us to keep on being highly ambitious for the future of early education and childcare and to make sure that we 'let children get their feet wet'. At first sight, that seems a strange thing to say: surely we want to do everything we can to keep children safe, secure – and dry? But, if we are taking children out on Forest School, and we want them to have a real outdoors experience and splash through puddles and go through sticky mud, then perhaps there will be the odd time when the water trickles over the top of their little wellington boots. Of course, no-one wants cold, wet and miserable children. But, equally, if we just keep to the dry ground and restrict children to playgrounds in the park with their safety surfaces, will children ever have the sorts of fantastic and rich experiences that we all need as part of our learning? Likewise, if we just keep to the safety surface of our own practice, we will be unable to innovate and we will not be providing the very best for the children in our care. Teams of professionals are not content to tick boxes and merely comply with other people's expected standards. They are not afraid to develop promising practice and find out that, when they look in detail at the outcomes, the venture has not been as successful as they had hoped and needs rethinking. Teams of professionals are prepared to experiment: they can tolerate some failures as they strive to improve.

The poet W.B. Yeats wrote that: 'education is not the filling of a pail, but the lighting of a fire'. We need to light that fire, because we need to inspire strong practitioners and future leaders, and we need the next generation of children to be strong, resilient, happy, well educated and well prepared for the future.

REFERENCES

Beere, J. (2010) *The Perfect Ofsted Lesson*. Bancyfelin: Independent Thinking Press.

Brown, B. (1998) *Unlearning Discrimination in the Early Years*. Stoke-on-Trent: Trentham.

Bruce, T. (2015) *Early Childhood Education*. London: Hodder Education.

Bullyonline (2004) 'UK National Workplace Bullying Advice Line: History and Statistics'. http://bullyonline.org/old/workbully/worbal.htm. Last accessed 28 May 2016.

Coe, R., Aloisi, C., Higgins, S. and Elliot Major, L. (2014) *What Makes Great Teaching? Review of the Underpinning Research*. London: Sutton Trust. www.suttontrust. com/wp-content/uploads/2014/10/What-makes-great-teaching-FINAL-4.11.14.pdf. Last accessed 28 May 2016.

Department for Education (DfE) (2011) *Supporting Families in the Foundation Years*. www. gov.uk/government/uploads/system/uploads/attachment_data/file/184868/DFE-01001-2011_supporting_families_in_the_foundation_years.pdf. Last accessed 28 May 2016.

DfE (2014) *Statutory Framework for the Early Years Foundation Stage: Setting the Standards for Learning, Development and Care for Children from Birth to Five*. www.gov.uk/government/ uploads/system/uploads/attachment_data/file/335504/EYFS_framework_from_1_ September_2014__with_clarification_note.pdf. Last accessed 28 May 2016.

DfE (2016) *Reception Baseline Comparability Study*. www.gov.uk/government/publications/ reception-baseline-comparability-study. Last accessed 28 May 2016.

Dweck, C. (2006) *Mindset: How You Can Fulfil Your Potential*. New York: Random House.

Early Education (2012) *Development Matters in the Early Years Foundation Stage (EYFS)*. www.early-education.org.uk/development-matters. Last accessed 28 May 2016.

Elfer, P. (2014) 'Social Defences in Nurseries'. In D. Armstrong and M.J. Rustin (eds) *Social Defences Against Anxiety: Explorations in the Paradigm* (Tavistock Clinic Series). London: Karnac.

Hargreaves, D.H. (2012) A Self-improving School System Towards Maturity. www. gov.uk/government/uploads/system/uploads/attachment_data/file/325908/a-self-improving-school-system-towards-maturity.pdf. Last accessed 28 May 2016.

Lane, J. (2008) *Young Children and Racial Justice*, 2nd edition. London: National Children's Bureau.

Nutbrown, C. (2012) *Foundations for Quality: The Independent Review of Early Education and Childcare Qualifications*. www.gov.uk/government/uploads/system/uploads/ attachment_data/file/175463/Nutbrown-Review.pdf. Last accessed 28 May 2016.

Ofsted (2013) *Getting it Right First Time: Achieving and Maintaining High-Quality Early Years Provision*. www.gov.uk/government/uploads/system/uploads/attachment_data/ file/418840/Getting_it_right_first_time.pdf. Last accessed 28 May 2016.

Ofsted (2015a) *Early Years Inspection Update*. www.gov.uk/government/uploads/ system/uploads/attachment_data/file/460566/Early_Years_Inspection_Update_ September_2015.pdf. Last accessed 28 May 2016.

Ofsted (2015b) *The Common Inspection Framework: Education, Skills and Early Years*. www.gov. uk/government/publications/common-inspection-framework-education-skills-and-early-years-from-september-2015. Last accessed 28 May 2016.

Ofsted (2015c) *Inspecting Safeguarding in Early Years, Education and Skills Settings*. www.gov. uk/government/uploads/system/uploads/attachment_data/file/457037/Inspecting_safe-guarding_in_early_years_education_and_skills_settings.pdf. Last accessed 28 May 2016.

Ofsted (2015d) *School Inspection Handbook*. www.gov.uk/government/uploads/system/uploads/attachment_data/file/458866/School_inspection_handbook_section_5_from_September_2015.pdf. Last accessed 28 May 2016.

Ofsted (2015e) *Early Years Inspection Handbook*. https://www.gov.uk/government/uploads/system/uploads/attachment_data/file/458588/Early_years_inspection_handbook.pdf. Last accessed 28 May 2016.

Pascal, C. and Bertram, T. (1997) *Effective Early Learning*. London: Sage.

Pask, R. and Joy, B. (2007) *Mentoring–Coaching: A Guide for Education Professionals*. Milton Keynes: Open University Press.

Plymouth Safeguarding Children Board (2010) *Serious Case Review: Overview Report, Executive Summary*. www.plymouth.gov.uk/serious_case_review_nursery_z.pdf. Last accessed 28 May 2016.

Siraj, I., Kingston, D. and Melhuish, E. (2015) *Assessing Quality in Early Childhood Education and Care*. Stoke-on-Trent: Trentham.

Siraj-Blatchford, I. (1994) *The Early Years: Laying the Foundations for Racial Equality.* Stoke-on-Trent: Trentham.

Starr, J. (2004) 'The manager's role in coaching: Overcoming barriers to success'. *Development and Learning in Organizations: An International Journal*, 18(2): 9–12.

Stewart, W. (2013) 'There is no right way to teach, says Ofsted chief inspector in exclusive *TES* interview'. *Times Educational Supplement*. www.tes.com/news/school-news/breaking-news/there-no-right-way-teach-says-ofsted-chief-inspector-exclusive-tes. Last accessed 28 May 2016.

Sylva, K., Melhuish, E., Sammons, P., Siraj-Blatchford, I. and Taggart, B. (eds) (2010) *Early Childhood Matters: Evidence from the Effective Pre-School and Primary Education Project*. London: Routledge.

The Telegraph (2014) 'NHS care watchdog warns of "alarming" culture'. www.telegraph.co.uk/news/nhs/10612450/NHS-care-watchdog-warns-of-alarming-culture.html. Last accessed 28 May 2016.

Tickell, C. (2011) *The Early Years: Foundations for Life, Health and Learning: An Independent Report on the Early Years Foundation Stage to Her Majesty's Government*. www.gov.uk/government/uploads/system/uploads/attachment_data/file/180919/DFE-00177-2011.pdf. Last accessed 28 May 2016.

INDEX